Country
Wisdom

Jerry Mack Johnson grew up in the ranch country of West Texas and during his lifetime has been a miner and prospector, merchant seaman, ranch hand, professional bull rider and rodeo clown, oilfield worker, salesman, agriculturist, and schoolteacher. He currently resides in San Angelo, Texas, where he is the vice-president of Supreme Feed Mills, Inc. He is the author of *What It's Worth and Where You Can Sell It: The Collector's Marketplace*, *The Catfish Farming Handbook*, and numerous articles on marketing, crop, and livestock production.

Country Wisdom

by

Jerry Mack Johnson

Anchor Press/Doubleday

Garden City, New York

1974

JH BIA

The Anchor Press edition is the first publication of *Country Wisdom* in book form. It is published simultaneously in hard and paper covers.

Anchor Press edition: 1974

Library of Congress Cataloging in Publication Data

Mack, Jerry.
  Country wisdom.

  SUMMARY: An almanac of rural lore, nature facts, and other "country wisdom" concerning the weather, moon, livestock, medicine, and other topics.

  1. Folk-lore—United States—Juvenile literature.
[1. Folk-lore—United States]   I. Title.
GR105.M32   390'.0973
ISBN 0-385-09638-0
Library of Congress Catalog Card Number 74–5529

DEDICATION

This book is joyfully dedicated to Mother Nature and to all that makes up Her better way of living.

to:

. . . the homestead
. . . the smell of new plowed ground
. . . sleeping on a pallet cause the house is full of folks you like
. . . newborn goats, lambs, and calves
. . . a fish jumping in the pond
. . . fluffy chicks and goslings
. . . a newly sprouted seed
. . . the blooming fruit tree
. . . Spring, with all its newness of Life
. . . tree leaves in the fall
. . . the first snow of winter
. . . a watermelon in the summer
. . . geese flying south
. . . finding a hidden stream
. . . a bird stopping for a drink near you
. . . a few fleecy white clouds in a deep blue sky
. . . the breeze that stirs the crisp new curtains in the kitchen in the summer
. . . ducks flying to the north country
. . . a small waterfall in the woods

Dedication

. . . birds singing at the crack of dawn

. . . the first buds to open on a tree

. . . the taste of hot pie in the country

. . . morning sunshine spilling across your breakfast

. . . eating a peach right off the tree

. . . a cold drink of water from a deep well on a hot summer day

. . . seeing an old friend who's been gone a long time

. . . making a new friend

. . . doing something for somebody just cause you want to

. . . washing your face in a fresh clear stream

. . . eating something cooked over a campfire

. . . the smell of fresh spring rain

. . . the arrival of your favorite season

. . . hot cornbread and country butter

. . . pulling up a homemade quilt on a cold winter night

. . . the smell of fresh coffee perking

. . . buying seeds and planning a garden

. . . having to choose between preserves, good sorghum, or wild honey

. . . a crocus breaking through the snow

. . . counting the new jars of vegetables and fruit put up in the fall

. . . staying home on your own land

and . . . to all that *you* hold near and dear to your heart!

A Special Dedication

To the many country folks, covering thousands of miles and several generations, who made the information in this book available to me.

CONTENTS

WITHDRAWN

INTRODUCTION

Mother Nature is trying to tell *you* something!

It is written in the Bible "be still and know that I am God." Nature says "be still and look at me. Listen to me for I have many things to show you and tell you." Every day, every hour, every minute nature is talking to each of us. We only need to look and listen.

She talks to us about our every endeavor. She talks to the farmer about his crops, the rancher about his livestock, the gardener about his plants, the sailor about the sea, the outdoorsman about the woods, the fisherman about the fish. She talks to all of us.

There is no work of man that cannot be aided by the proper reading of Mother Nature's signs. There is no difficulty or problem that nature does not supply the answer. We must be still and listen. Some answers we do not know; we have not yet listened closely enough.

On this very day some of the world's most renowned medical scientists are probing remote areas of the globe to learn secrets of nature about curing disease that primitive peoples have uncovered. Secrets that we, with all our technology, have not discovered. Every day we learn more and more about ourselves and our environment as we open our eyes and our ears to nature's many signs.

This book covers the signs of the zodiac and the phases of the moon that country people have used for many years. It also contains the wisdom about many of nature's signs that has been passed from generation to generation by word of mouth from folks in every corner of our country. It is the folklore on which America was raised. Although this book by no means contains all the signs that have been passed down to us, it is a representative sample of many of them.

Read and use those that are here. Look and listen for more. Mother Nature has some things she would like to say only to *you*.

JERRY MACK JOHNSON
San Angelo, Texas

Country Wisdom

Each day foretells the next,
If one could read the signs;
Today is the progenitor of tomorrow.

—JOHN BURROUGHS, 1900

Chapter 1

WEATHER

At times it is nice to have advance knowledge of what Mother Nature has in mind for tomorrow's weather. By reading her weather signs you can become a fairly reliable weather forecaster.

Frank Reed of Cleveland, Georgia, became famous as a mountain weather prognosticator in 1960. Many of the city newspapers carried stories about him. On March 1 of that year, just a few days before spring, he had predicted that winter wasn't over and that the worst was yet to come. He was right. Three severe snow storms covered the Southeast during that March, completely isolating whole areas. In 1972 he was right again when he predicted that it would be a mighty cold winter—it proved to be one of the worst in this nation's history.

He predicted both of these bad winters by his close observation of various signs in nature. He noticed that the hair on calves' necks became thick and shaggy in the fall prior to these paralyzing winters. He also made a careful study of corn shucks. He says that when they are extra thick and tight it means a rough, cold winter.

Some of Frank's other observations are: dry weather comes when a mule rolls in the dirt and then shakes the dirt off; a sure sign of a storm is when cats run and play in the house; and it generally means rain when the leaves on a tree turn "bottom side up" in the summertime.

Some Indian tribes in the Midwest could always predict a severe winter by the development of flanges or fringes on the toes of ruffed grouse. These made their feet more like snowshoes for the big snows that were on the way. Indians also watched for animals growing a short coat under a heavier than usual growth of fur or hair as a sure sign of a bad winter ahead.

Old range riders in the Southwest knew a blizzard was coming when the coyotes would move close to their camps and stay around them day and night.

Early farm folks even predicted complete seasons: "A year of snow, a year of plenty." They reasoned that a cold, snowy winter prevented premature blossoming of fruit trees and, thus, the chance of the blossoms being nipped by a late freeze was less. It also lessened the chance of wheat and other early grains being damaged by late frost.

Some forecasters feel that the first twelve days after Christmas tell what the weather will be during each month of the next year. Cullen Cole in Texas made his predictions for the full year from what he observed and recorded during the first twelve hours of the New Year.

What follows is a gathering of many of nature's weather signs that have been handed down for many generations. These are signs learned on the range, prairie, mountains, and sea. We have gathered them over many years and many miles.

CLOUDS

> Sometime we see a cloud that's dragonish;
> A vapour sometime like a bear or lion,
> A towered citadel, a pendent rock,
> A forked mountain, or blue promontory
> With trees upon't, that nod unto the world
> And mock our eyes with air . . . .
> That which is now a horse, even with a thought
> The rack dislimns and makes it indistinct,
> As water is in water.
>
> —SHAKESPEARE, *Antony and Cleopatra*

Clouds are so often with us we usually overlook them unless a storm is on the way. Mother Nature has a habit of using clouds to write messages in the sky, plain enough for all to see, about what She plans to do with the weather. There are two basic cloud formations; "cumulus" clouds, which are puffy or piled up, and are formed by rising air currents, and "stratus," which are layered or sheetlike clouds. Stratus clouds are formed when a layer of air is cooled below saturation level without any vertical movement. There are also four families of clouds: high, middle, low, and towering clouds.

The "Summary of Cloud Types" that follows will help you identify the major cloud types and better understand their relationship to the weather.

3

SUMMARY OF CLOUD TYPES

Height	Cloud Name and Symbol	Description
High Clouds (16,500 to 45,000 ft.)	Cirrus (Ci)	Thin, feathery, white, whispy, with silky edges. Semi-transparent. Form at great heights. The first clouds to show color before sunrise and the last to darken at or after sunset.
	Cirrocumulus (Cc)	Lumpy, fibrous small bands. Often called "mackerel sky." Rippled to look like sand on the beach. Wave-like appearance.
	Cirrostratus (Cs)	Thin milky veil with whitish haze. Does not obscure but often produces halo around sun or moon. Sometimes called "mare's tail" clouds.

Height	Cloud Name and Symbol	Description
Middle Clouds (6,500 to 35,000 ft.)	Altocumulus (Ac)	Patches or layers of fluffy roll-like clouds. Usually arranged in rows. One form is "sheep's back," which looks like a layer of cotton balls. Another form appears as long bands or rolls of cotton crowded together.
	Altostratus (As)	Heavy gray sheet or gray film, lightly striped. Almost obscures the sun or moon like viewing through a heavy, frosted glass. Causes a corona or soft luminous circle on the edge of the sun or moon.
	Nimbostratus (Ns)	Form beneath altostratus. Have a wet look. Low formless dark clouds of bad weather. Ragged rain clouds.

Country Wisdom

Height	Cloud Name and Symbol	Description
Low Clouds (0 to 6,500 ft.)	Stratocumulus (Sc)	Series of gray patches of roll-like clouds. Has shadow effect. Fluffy and wavy surface. Long, flattened puffs.
	Stratus (St)	Lowest of clouds. Shapeless, smooth layer with foglike appearance. Often form heavy leaden sky. If broken into shreds are called fractostratus.
Towering Clouds (range from low to highest levels, caused by strong vertical wind currents)	Cumulus (Cu)	Puffy, billowy, changeable, thick clouds. Usually scattered over a fair weather sky.
	Cumulonimbus (Cb)	Typical "thunderhead." Often with flat horizontal bases and tops that are flat anvil-like. Pile to great heights. Strong light shadows.

Forecasting Weather by the Clouds

HIGH CLOUDS

If clouds are white and thin and scattered across the sky with mostly west winds, the weather will be fair with little change.

It is a strong indication of rain if clouds turn gray or show yellow coloring and thicken, seemingly moving together; if they gradually drop and thick clouds develop beneath them; if the high clouds move from the south or from the southwest with surface winds prevailing from the east. There will be some wind and visibility will be reduced; rain will begin in six to twenty-four hours. Winds will usually shift to the southwest and will be warmer.

Cirrostratus are responsible for "halo rings" around the sun or moon. If they thicken it is a strong indication of coming snow or rain.

MIDDLE CLOUDS

There is a good possibility of rain within six to twelve hours when these clouds change from patches into layers and blankets; if their movement is from the south or southwest with surface wind prevailing from the east; if a "corona" or soft luminous circle forms on the edge of the sun or moon. The weather will later change to warmer temperatures and it will be partly cloudy with winds from the southwest.

If the clouds remain apart and open blue sky can be seen between the cloud patches, or if the clouds are moving in the same general direction as the surface wind is blowing, there will be little or no change in the weather and it will remain fair.

7

If the cloud patches are swiftly moving from the west or from the northwest, or if surface winds are from the south or southwest, there is a possibility of quick showers, hard but of short duration. The wind will shift to come from the northwest and it will be clear with cooler temperatures.

If the cloud patches are noticeable about midmorning during the humid part of summer or if the clouds have high-peaked humps coming from a broad base there will be gusty winds soon with a good possibility of thunderstorms.

When the sun becomes hazy, surface winds are from the east or southeast, and the altostratus layers become lower and darken, especially in the south or southwest, be prepared for continuous and steady rain in a short while. This will be followed by warm southwest winds.

LOW CLOUDS

If stratocumulus clouds come together creating an overcast with much gray coloring, there is a very good chance of rain.

When stratocumulus clouds appear puffed with open blue sky showing between the patches and the clouds move in the same general direction as the surface wind there will be no change in the weather for twenty-four to forty-eight hours.

If there is a heavy, thick stratocumulus covering that continues to rise higher and crumbles and breaks in places when the wind is from the west, you can expect cooler temperatures and clearing.

When a stratocumulus cloud bank that is rolled and very long shows in the west or northwest with strong surface winds prevailing from the south or southwest, there is a good possibility of short, sudden, hard rain storms. These will be followed by clear weather with lower temperatures.

When there are higher, stratus clouds in the morning and surface winds are light, these clouds will soon break and the sky will become clear.

Low, heavy stratus clouds forming a heavy, leaden sky frequently cause only drizzle, especially in valleys and along coastlines.

When dark nimbostratus clouds form from low altostratus clouds with movement from the south or southwest while surface winds prevail from the southeast, there is almost a 100 per cent probability of steady rain. This will be followed by warmer weather when the clouds break up and the wind will then prevail from the south or southwest.

TOWERING CLOUDS

When cumulus clouds float alone in a blue sky, especially in the afternoon, you can expect fair weather and a break-up of the clouds by sunset.

When cumulus clouds form about midmorning or a little later, especially on a humid day, and continue to build rapidly by midafternoon, there will be thundershowers, usually in the late afternoon or evening.

When cumulonimbus clouds build in separate masses and drift in from the south or southwest, there will be sharp winds from the south and southwest. There should be thunderstorms in the later afternoon and evening, and there might also be hail and short, hard gusting winds.

Watch for heavy cumulus or cumulonimbus clouds forming in solid banks in the west, northwest, and north. Surface winds will be strong from the south or southwest, and there are strong possibilities of severe thunderstorms, with squall lines moving through the area and wind prevailing from the west or northwest. This will be followed by cooler temperatures and clearing skys.

Particular attention should be paid to heavy cumulonimbus clouds that develop with very dark, billowy bottoms. They usually have a roll cloud at the forward lower edge, building both downward and to great heights upward and are breeders of our most severe weather. Watch for hard thunderstorms, damaging hail, high winds with turbulence, and be prepared to seek shelter from tornadoes.

. . . More Cloud Reading

◆ Hard-edged clouds mean wind.

◆ Delicate, soft-looking clouds tell of fine weather with moderate to high breezes.

◆ A gloomy, dark but very blue sky says windy but fair.

◆ A bright yellowness of the clouds at sunset foretells wind; a pale yellow color means rain.

◆ The softer the look of the clouds the less wind there will be. Hard-looking clouds with rolled and ragged appearance tell of coming strong wind.

◆ Small ink-colored clouds speak of rain.

◆ Light, skimming clouds driving across and beneath heavy masses show wind and rain, or sometimes just wind, depending on the type of cloud cover above them.

◆ High clouds crossing in a direction different from the lower cloud cover foretell of a wind change in the direction of their drift.

◆ After a period of fair weather, the first signs of a coming change are usually light streaks, wisps, or light patches of white, distant clouds. These increase and are followed by a murky vapor that develops into clouds. This is an almost infallible sign of approaching wind and rain. The higher and more distant these indicators start the more gradual, but more complete, will be the change.

◆ Light delicate tints of color in clouds of soft texture indicate fine weather. Sharp, distinct colors in harder, more distinct clouds are forerunners of rain and strong winds.

SIGNS OF WIND

◆ Soft, vapory, and widely extended redness in the east in the early morning means wind.

◆ If, just before the sun rises, there appears at the point of rising a rosy column shooting straight upward like a shaft of deeply dyed vapor, and if the base of the column glows like the sun itself, be prepared for a very windy day.

◆ Clouds that look like a horse's tail when it is running mean strong winds.

◆ Sharp horns on the moon foretell strong winds.

◆ North wind brings cooler weather; south wind brings warmer weather.

◆ Expect wind in the morning when an evening sky is yellow.

◆ A high dawn, look for wind. (A "high dawn" occurs when the first indications of daylight are seen above a bank of clouds.)

◆ "When the wind veers against the sun,
   Trust it not, for back 'twill run."

◆ "Mackerel sky and mare's tails,
   Make lofty ships carry low sails."

◆ "If clouds look as if scratched by a hen,
   Get ready to reef your topsails then."

◆ "When the wind is in the South
   The rain is in it's mouth,
   When the wind is in the East
   It's neither good for man nor beast,
   The wind in the West
   Suits everyone best."

Estimating Wind Speeds by the Beaufort Scale

In 1805, Admiral Beaufort of the British Navy composed a
scale that estimated wind speeds from their effects on ships sails.
His scale is changed here for use on land.

Beaufort Number	Miles per Hour	Knots	Description	Visible Sign
0	0–1	0–1	Calm	Smoke rises skyward
1	1–3	1–3	Light air	Smoke slowly drifts
2	4–7	4–6	Light breeze	Tree leaves rustle
3	8–12	7–10	Gentle breeze	Tree leaves and twigs move

Beaufort Number	Miles per Hour	Knots	Description	Visible Sign
4	13–18	11–16	Moderate breeze	Small branches of trees move
5	19–24	17–21	Fresh breeze	Small trees sway
6	25–31	22–27	Strong breeze	Large tree branches sway
7	32–38	28–33	Moderate gale	Whole trees sway
8	39–46	34–40	Fresh gale	Twigs break from trees
9	47–54	41–47	Strong gale	Tree branches break
10	55–63	48–55	Full gale	Whole trees snap or blow down
11	64–72	56–63	Storm	Violent storm— much damage
12	73–82	64–71	Hurricane	Severe destruction

SIGNS OF RAIN

◆ Leaves turn over and show their bottom sides before a rain.

◆ Red sunrise with clouds lowering later in the morning tells of rain.

◆ A south wind brings rain.

◆ Winds from the east bring wet weather.

◆ Watch for rain when distant sounds are loud and sharp.

◆ Rain with an east wind is of long duration.

- When smoke is sluggish in rising be prepared for wet weather.

- Rain can come when the quarter moon is tipping downward.

- Sudden rain is of short duration. Slow rain lasts a long time.

- High clouds won't bring rain.

- A strip of seaweed in the house stays dry and dusty-like in fine weather; with rains on the way it gets damp and sticky.

- Night cloudiness in patches foretells rain. "When the stars begin to huddle, the earth will soon become a puddle."

- Big rains usually begin about midmorning.

- If there is a thunderstorm before noon on any day in September you can expect much rain and snow through the winter.

- If the sun comes out while it is raining, it will rain the next day.

- A gray sunset with lowering clouds or one in which the sky is green or yellowish-green indicates rain.

- A morning rainbow is a sign of rain.

- "Rain before seven, quits before eleven."

- Rain on Sunday means some rain during the next week.

- "The moon with a circle brings water in her back."

- "If the moon shows a silver shield,
  Be not afraid to reap your field,
  But if she rises haloed round,
  Soon we'll tread on deluged ground."

◆ "Rain long foretold, long last,
  Short notice, soon past."

◆ "When grass is dry in morning light,
  Look for rain before the night,
  When dew is on the grass,
  Rain will never come to pass."

◆ "When ye see a cloud rise out of the west, straightway
  cometh the rain; and so it is."—Luke 12:54

◆ "Mackerel sky, mackerel sky,
  Not long wet, nor yet long dry."

◆ "If the sun goes pale to bed,
  'Twill rain tomorrow, it is said."

◆ "An evening gray and morning red,
  Will send the shepherd wet to bed."

HOW TO JUDGE THE DISTANCE OF A THUNDERSTORM

Light travels at about 186,000 miles per second. Sound travels at roughly 1,100 feet per second. This means that sound travels about 1 mile in 5 seconds. To judge how far a thunderstorm is from you, you must time how long it takes the sound of thunder to reach you after you see the lightning flash. By counting "1,001, 1,002, 1,003, 1,004, 1,005," at normal speed you can count seconds. Using this system, if you can count from 1,001 to 1,010 at normal speed from the time you see the lightning until you hear the thunder, you know the thunderstorm is about two miles away.

A thunderstorm usually announces its appearance by a sudden blast of cold air that flows over the ground ahead of the rain and storm. This cold blast usually precedes the storm by about three miles.

HOW MUCH RAIN FELL?

To have an idea of the amount of rain water that falls on an acre of ground, the following should be of interest:

0.01 inch	of rain equals			62,726	cubic inches or			1.1 tons
0.05 "	"	"	"	313,632	"	"	"	5.6 "
0.10 "	"	"	"	627,264	"	"	"	11.3 "
1.00 "	"	"	"	6,272,640	"	"	"	113.0 "
2.00 inches	"	"	"	12,545,280	"	"	"	226.0 "
5.00 inches	"	"	"	31,363,200	"	"	"	565.0 "

The number of inches of snow that corresponds to 1 inch of water is not constant due to variations in the texture of snow. It can vary from 6 inches to 25, but a good average is about 10 inches of snow equals 1 inch of water.

SIGNS OF STORM

◆ When the atmosphere is telescopic, and distant objects (the stars at night, for instance) stand out unusually clear and sharp, a storm could be near. So, too, for sounds: "Sound traveling far and wide, a stormy day will betide."

- Broad, deep, and angry redness in the east in the early morning means storm.

- Clouds are sometimes not so indicative of a storm as the total absence of clouds when other signs prevail.

- An obscured sunset after a bright day foretells a storm.

- A growing whiteness in the sky tells of an approaching storm.

- When the needles of pine trees turn west there will be heavy snow.

- Red sky in the morning is usually a storm warning.

- Halos or sun dogs are large circles, or parts of circles, around the sun or moon. When they occur after fine weather it indicates stormy weather will follow.

- Storms, rain, and snow may come when the barometer falls steadily.

- Storms come often when the south wind increases in speed with clouds moving from the west.

- A dark, threatening western sky indicates storm.

- A wind shift in a counterclockwise direction, as from north to west, indicates a storm or rain, especially when it starts as a north wind.

- "Evening red and morning gray
  Sends the traveler on his way,
  Evening gray and morning red
  Brings rain down on his head."

- "Rainbow at night, shepherd's delight
  Rainbow in morning, shepherd's warning."

SIGNS OF FAIR WEATHER

◆ If just before sunrise the undersides of the eastern clouds turn to pink or rose and eventually the whole sky flushes, fair weather will always follow.

◆ A clear sunset is a sign of good weather.

◆ A rainbow in the evening says fair weather will follow.

◆ Soft, fluffy clouds means fine weather to come.

◆ Wind from the west brings fine weather.

◆ Good weather comes with high clouds.

◆ A steady or rising barometer means fair weather.

◆ The weather will remain fair when fluffy cumulus clouds dot the afternoon summer sky.

◆ When morning fog "burns off" or disappears by noon, expect a fair weather day.

◆ "Red sky in the morning
Is the sailor's sure warning,
Red sky at night
Is the sailor's delight."

◆ "Rainbow to windward, foul falls the day;
Rainbow to leeward, rain runs away."

◆ "Do business with men when the wind is from the north-west." (There is often a link between weather and human behavior. In this case, when the weather is most likely to be fair, people tend to be in better spirits and easier to deal with.)

SIGNS OF DRY WEATHER

◆ Heavy dew in the early mornings means that dry weather will follow.

◆ A north wind brings dry air.

◆ A dry summer will follow a winter with few storms and blizzards.

SIGNS OF TEMPERATURE CHANGE

◆ Temperature will fall when the wind blows from the north or northwest or shifts to the north or northwest.

◆ Temperature will fall when the night sky is clear and the wind is light.

◆ Temperature will fall in the winter when the barometer rises steadily.

◆ Temperature will rise when the wind is from the south, especially with a cloud cover at night or clear sky during the day.

SIGNS OF SPRING AND SUMMER

◆ When trees split their bark in the winter, it will be a dry, hot spring.

- Thunderstorms that come before seven in the morning in April and May foretell a wet summer.

- When snowdrifts face to the north, spring will arrive early.

- When the hay in the fields leans to the northeast, summer will be long and hot.

SIGNS OF FALL AND WINTER

- When tree leaves drop early, the fall will be short and winter will be mild.

- When the tree leaves fall late, winter will be severe.

- A late frost means a long, hard winter.

- Two frosts mean winter will soon appear.

- The longer and hotter the summer, the longer and colder the winter. Extremes breed extremes.

- If the moss on the north side of a tree dries up in the fall it is to be a mild winter.

- If the husks of corn and nuts grow thick and tight, the winter will be hard.

- Rolling thunder in the fall means a hard winter.

- The first frost will occur six months after the first thunder of spring.

- Sun dogs in the winter means cold weather ahead.

- "Clear moon, frost soon." (Moonlight nights bring the heaviest frosts.)

◆ "If Candlemas Day be bright and clear,
   We'll have two winters in the year."

◆ "If on the trees the leaves still hold,
   The coming winter will be cold."

FORECASTING WEATHER BY THE MOON

"This table and the accompanying remarks are the results of many years of actual observation, the whole being constructed on a due consideration of the attraction of the Sun and Moon, in their several positions respecting the Earth, and will, by simple inspection, show the observer what kind of weather will most probably follow the entrance of the Moon into any of its quarters, and that so near the truth, as to be seldom or never found to fail."

—FRANCIS H. BUZZACOTT, The Complete American and Canadian Sportsman's Encyclopedia of Valuable Instruction, 1913

If the new moon, first quarter, full moon, or last quarter, occurs:	In Summer:	In Winter:
Between midnight and 2 A.M.	Fair	Frost, unless wind southwest
2 and 4 A.M.	Cold and showers	Snow and stormy
4 and 6 A.M.	Rain	Rain
6 and 8 A.M.	Wind and rain	Stormy

If the new moon, first quarter, full moon, or last quarter, occurs:	In Summer:	In Winter:
8 and 10 A.M.	Changeable	Cold rain if wind from the west, snow if from the east
10 and 12 A.M.	Frequent showers	Cold and high wind
12 and 2 P.M.	Very rainy	Snow or rain
2 and 4 P.M.	Changeable	Fair and mild
4 and 6 P.M.	Fair	Fair
6 and 8 P.M.	Fair if wind northwest	Fair and frosty if wind north or northeast
8 and 10 P.M.	Rainy if south or southwest wind	Rain or snow if south or southwest wind
10 and midnight	Fair	Fair and frosty

A BAROMETER FOR GENERAL FORECASTING

We deal mostly with natural signs from nature without the use of equipment or instruments. A barometer, however, is a good mechanical device for helping you be more accurate in your weather forecasting from signs. A dependable, inexpensive barometer can be purchased from most hardware stores. Before using your new instrument you must calibrate it to sea-level pressures. This can be done free of charge by checking with your nearest weather station or airport.

Use the following chart to determine your general forecast. It is wise to keep a record of your forecasts determined from this chart and of actual local weather changes. This way you can soon learn how your local weather fits with this chart and make allowances accordingly.

Wind is from:	Barometric or Atmospheric Pressure:	General Forecast Indicated:
SW to NW	30.10 to 30.20 barometer steady	Fair, little temperature change for 24 to 48 hours.
SW to NW	30.10 to 30.20 rising rapidly	Fair, warmer weather; rain possible within 48 hours.
SW to NW	30.20 or above barometer steady	Continued fair; little change in temperature.
SW to NW	30.20 or above falling slowly	Fair, slowly rising temperatures for about 48 hours.
S to SE	30.10 to 30.20 falling slowly	Increasing wind; rain possible within 24 hours.
S to SE	30.10 to 30.20 falling rapidly	Rain within 12 to 24 hours. Rising wind.
SE to NE	30.10 to 30.20 falling slowly	Rain within 12 to 18 hours. Rising wind.
SE to NE	30.10 to 30.20 falling rapidly	Rain within 12 hours. Rising wind.
SE to NE	30.00 or below falling slowly	Rain to continue for 24 hours or more.
SE to NE	30.00 or below falling rapidly	High wind and rain in a few hours. Clearing in 36 hours—colder in winter.

Wind is from:	Barometric or Atmospheric Pressure:	General Forecast Indicated:
E to NE	30.10 or above falling slowly	In summer, with light winds there will be rain in 2 to 4 days. In winter, rain or snow in 24 hours.
E to NE	30.10 or above falling rapidly	In summer, rain possible in 12 to 24 hours. In winter, rain or snow in 12 hours.
S to SW	30.00 or below rising slowly	Clearing in a few hours. Fair for several days.
S to E	29.80 or below falling rapidly	Severe storm in a few hours, clearing in 24 hours. Colder in winter.
E to N	29.80 or below falling rapidly	Severe storm in a few hours. Heavy rains or snowstorm. Winter cold wave.
Turning to W	29.80 or below rising rapidly	End of storm. Colder and clear.

WHAT DEW, FROST, AND DEW POINT TELL US

The amount of dew depends on the coolness of the weather and on the type of surface upon which it collects. Some objects such as cotton, fur, silk, vegetables, and wool, collect dew more readily than others. Sand, gravel, rocks, and cement do not collect much dew. It seems that Mother Nature allows dew to collect upon the things that can benefit most from its refreshing influence. Dew seldom, if ever, collects during cloudy nights.

The "dew point" as indicated by a hygrometer (which can be purchased from most hardware stores) can be used in the evening to foretell the lowest temperature of the coming night. By determining the dew point, an approaching low temperature or frost can be forecast and proper precautions for vegetation and livestock can be taken. When the dew point appears below freezing level, frost will form instead of dew.

A heavy dew in the morning is a sure sign of fine weather for that day. As dew is not formed during heavy cloudiness and wind it is almost proof positive of fair weather ahead.

Hoar frost (a silver-white deposit of ice needles usually perpendicular to the objects on which they occur) is a sure sign of changeable weather.

WHAT PLANTS TELL US ABOUT THE WEATHER

Plants talk to us about the various needs they have while they are growing. They also give us a few things to consider about the weather, especially concerning the type of fall and winter we can expect.

Mose Spooner of Colquitt, Georgia, always said that when the berry bushes bloomed heavily and produced their crop earlier than usual you better watch out for a rough winter. He was nearly always right. Some prophets of winter weather say they go only by the nut crop. Acorn, hickory, and pecan nuts grow thick, tight husks around an extra heavy shell when a bad winter is on the way.

You need to watch for fruit trees and other bearing plants that seem to produce their harvest earlier than usual. In most cases they will have a larger than usual crop too. This forewarns of early severe winter weather.

Root crops such as carrots, onions, and turnips grow deeper before a severe winter. Onions have more layers and other root plants, such as potatoes, have tougher skins.

Always watch the trees. Before a bad winter their bark is thicker than usual, especially on the north side, and the leaves stay on until very late in the fall.

In West Texas the threat of a killing frost is never past until the mesquite tree puts out its leaves. Sometimes even it gets caught but not often. It's the best sign that spring is really here for us. There is a tree in your part of the country that is just as reliable—you need to ask one of the old-timers which one it is.

WHAT ANIMALS, BIRDS, AND INSECTS TELL US ABOUT THE WEATHER

◆ Busy spiders mean the weather will be fine.

◆ Spiders hiding and breaking webs warn of a coming storm.

◆ Flies bite hard before a storm.

◆ When birds ruffle their feathers and huddle together watch for rain.

◆ When pack rats build nests with much height to them in the summer be prepared for a severe winter.

- When swallows are seen flying high it is an indication of good weather. The insects upon which they feed venture high only in the best weather.

- When chickens stay out in the rain, the rain will last all day.

- The darker the color of caterpillars in the fall, the harder the winter will be.

- Birds eat more just before a storm.

- When geese can walk on top of the snow in March, there will be a muddy spring.

- Bees are not good weather prophets as they will continue to leave the hive when a storm is imminent.

- A very reliable weather sign is given by ants. They often bring their eggs up out of their underground retreats and expose them to the warmth of the sun to be hatched. When they are seen carrying them in again in great haste, beware of a coming storm.

- When cattle and horses stay in close groups, a storm is coming.

- When birds fly low, there will be much snow (or rain).

- When birds stop singing, and trees start swinging, a storm is on its way.

- When it is hard to scare crows out of the corn field it will be a hard winter.

- When a cow bellers three times without stopping, a storm is coming.

- When fireflies are about in numbers, the weather will be fair for the next three days.

- Earthworms leave their holes in the ground and roam about when rains are coming.

- When the rooster crows at noon, rain will come soon.

- When ants build small hills, it will be a hot, dry summer.

- A sure sign of dry weather is horses and mules rolling in the dirt and shaking it off.

- Trout swimming in circles in the stream signifies a mild winter.

- Crickets singing in the house tell of a long, cold winter.

- Chattering squirrels tell of a mild winter. When squirrels do not chatter, and gather many nuts early in the fall, often green ones, expect a long, cold winter.

- When hornet and wasp nests are low and fat, winter will be hard.

- Extra fluffy squirrel's tails, and nests built low in trees, tell of a cold winter.

- Dogs sniffing the air frequently indicates a change in weather.

- Dogs bury more food and bones in the fall before a bad winter.

- Heavy coats of hair on dogs in the fall is a good sign of a long, hard winter.

- If in the fall dogs curl up in a ball by the fireplace to sleep it will be a bad winter.

◆ When the beaver adds more wood to the north side of his home, the winter will be long.

◆ Heavy fur on the bottom of the feet of rabbits foretell a cold winter.

◆ When butterflies migrate in the early fall, winter will come early.

◆ When horses sniff the air and gather in fence corners, it usually means a summer shower if there was no early morning dew.

FALSE WEATHER SIGNS

There are signs that are thought to be reliable that often are not, because the area of coverage is too great. Some farmers look upon the Milky Way as a weather vane, and will tell you that the way it points at night indicates the direction of the wind the next day. So, also, every new moon is either a dry moon or a wet moon. Dry if a hat would hang on the lower point, wet if it would not. They forget the fact that, as a rule, when it is dry in one part of the continent it is wet in some other part, and vice versa.

When the farmer kills his hogs in the fall, if the pork is hard and solid he predicts a severe winter; if soft and loose he predicts the opposite. Overlooked is the fact that the type of feed the hog has eaten and the temperature of the fall makes the pork hard or soft. So, too, with a hundred other signs, all the result of hasty or incomplete observations.

John Burroughs, in his book entitled *Signs and Seasons,* said: "One season, the last day of December was very warm. The bees were out of the hive, and there was no frost in the air or on the ground. I was walking in the woods, and as I paused in the shade of a hemlock tree I heard a sound from beneath the wet leaves on the ground but a few feet from me that suggested a frog. Following it cautiously, I at last determined the exact spot from whence the sound issued; lifting up the thick layer of leaves, there sat a frog—the wood frog, one of the first to appear in the marshes in spring, and which I have called the 'clucking frog'—in a little excavation in the surface of the ground. This, then, was its hibernaculum; here it was prepared to pass the winter, with only a coverlid of wet matted leaves between it and zero weather.

"Forthwith I became a prophet of warm weather, and among other things predicted a failure of the ice crop on the river; which, indeed, others who had not heard frogs croak on the 31st of December had also begun to predict. Surely, I thought, this frog knows what it is about; here is the wisdom of nature; it would have gone deeper into the ground than that if a severe winter was approaching; so I was not anxious about my coal bin, nor disturbed by longings for Florida. But what a winter followed! The winter of 1885, when the Hudson became coated with ice nearly two feet thick, and when March was as cold as January! I thought of my frog under the hemlock and wondered how it was faring. So one day the latter part of March, when the snow was gone, and there was a feeling of spring in the air, I turned aside in my walk to investigate it. The matted leaves were still frozen hard, but I succeeded in lifting them up and exposing the frog. There it sat as fresh and unscathed as in the fall. The ground beneath and all about it was still frozen like a rock, but apparently it had some means of its own of resisting the frost. It winked and bowed its head when I touched it, but did not seem inclined to leave its retreat. Some days later, after the frost was nearly all out of the ground, I passed that way, and found my frog had come out of its seclusion and was resting amid the dry leaves. There was not much jump in it yet, but its color was growing lighter. A few more warm days, and its fellows, and doubtless itself too, were croaking and gamboling in the marshes.

"This incident convinced me of two things; namely, that frogs know no more about the coming weather than we do, and that they do not retreat as deep into the ground to pass the winter as has been supposed. I used to think the muskrats could foretell an early and severe winter and have so written. But I am now convinced they cannot; they know as little about it as I do. Sometimes on an early and severe frost they seem to get alarmed and go to building their houses, but usually they seem to build early or late, high or low, just as the whim takes them.

"In most of the operations of nature there is at least one unknown quantity; to find the exact value of this unknown factor is not so easy. The fur of the animals, the feathers of the fowls, the husks of the maize, why are they thicker some seasons than others; what is the value of the unknown quantity here? Does it indicate a severe winter approaching? Only observations extending over a series of years can determine the point. How much patient observation it takes to settle many of the facts in the lives of the birds, animals, and insects!"

SPECIAL WEATHER SIGNS

There are a few points in reading the weather signs of nature that must be kept in mind at all times. These general rules were closely observed and followed by the most accurate early-day weather prognosticators. To improve your own forecasting skill always keep these in mind:

◆ In forecasting weather the critical moments of the day are sunrise and sunset.

◆ All weather signs fail in a drouth. The same theory is true during a wet spell. At these times nature is caught in a rut and reverses itself slowly.

◆ On most occasions the weather is very sure to declare itself by or before eleven o'clock in the morning. If the morning is unsettled wait until about eleven and you will know what the remainder of the day will be like. Other old-timers have said: "You can tell between eleven and two what the weather will do."

◆ Midday clouds and afternoon clouds, except in the season of thunderstorms, are usually harmless idlers and vagabonds. Pay little attention to them.

Chapter 2

MOON LORE

"It is well to remember that every living thing needs the
light of the moon and the light of the sun. The rays,
vibrations, and power of these two bodies differ but both
are needed in their own way."

—John Carroll

A few people laugh when you mention doing anything by the "signs." They con-
sider it to be the "old way," and surely couldn't be the "best
way." Oft times the old way has been tried, tested, and proved
by many people over long periods of time. The new way sometimes looks and sounds good but has not been put to the test of
time. We cannot say that all the information about moon signs
in this book is absolutely correct and one hundred per cent
foolproof. Some of it is fact and some of it is folklore and super-
stition, but it makes interesting reading and many of the old bits
of wisdom found here *have* stood the test of time. They might be
worth another try today.

Everything within the patterns of nature operates in cycles.
The study of these cycles has nothing to do with fortunetelling,
soothsaying, or mysticism. There is a harmony in nature. There
is a harmony between the sun, moon, stars, and the earth. This
information is derived from comparisons, investigations, and
studies made by men for centuries concerning the relationship

of things on this earth to the heavenly bodies above and about the earth. As we have just seen with the weather, when one thing happens in nature it foretells of other things that are about to happen. Proper study of certain events and what happens after they occur can help us in many of our day-to-day activities. There is a "best time" to do everything.

Folks who use the moon as their guide in farming and gardening believe that rhythm and timing are important in these activities. To be really successful with your farm, garden, or other enterprises using moon phases and signs, you must learn to set your pace with Mother Nature.

The time to break sod, to plant seed, to set out plants, to cultivate, to eradicate weeds and pests, to eliminate noxious growths, the time to harvest, the time to store the harvest, all come in due season with the timing and rhythm of the moon phases and the moon zodiac signs. Students of moon sign agricultural procedures believe there is a precise and special time for every chore to be done within the lunar year. This timing and rhythm exist on the broad scale of each month within the year. The same rhythm is found in the daily moon signs. By using the daily sign with the broad general signs that are in effect at a given time, proper timing and rhythm can be achieved in farming, gardening, and other activities.

There are many signs in nature that are quite obvious to us. We know that summer will follow spring, we know that winter will follow fall. By knowing this we will not plant crops that require heat in the wintertime. In this respect we understand nature and co-operate with her. She gives us many other signs that we should follow, many not as obvious as the signs of the seasons. If we will come into harmony with nature by knowing, studying, and reading her many signs we will live a better life, live easier, and enjoy life more.

THE PHASES OF THE MOON

The phases of the moon are caused by the varying angle at which its lighted surface is visible from the earth.

There are four moon phases. The new moon and the full moon are the most familiar and easiest to recognize. There are only two moon phases known as "quarters"; the "first quarter" and the "third (or last) quarter." They are both actually seen in the sky as half-moons. Numerous publications picture them as one quarter of a full moon and call them quarters but this is incorrect. The correct profile of each quarter is that of one half of the full moon. The team quarter refers not to the shape of the moon as it appears in the sky but to time elapsed between each twenty-eight-day "month."

On this basis the new moon is the start of the first half and the full moon is the start of the last half of the lunar month. Each of the four segments or phases has an approximate length of seven days. New moon to new moon is the full cycle of twenty-eight days. Knowing these moon phases *correctly* is the first step in learning moon lore and working with moon signs.

Moon Rise

◆ The new moon always rises with the sunrise in the east to start a new lunar month. The sun blots out the visibility of the new moon as it comes up but it can be seen as a thin crescent setting in the west at sunset a day or two after its rise.

◆ The first quarter (waxing) moon always rises about noon in the east seven days after the new moon and appears as a pale half-moon.

◆ The full moon always rises in the east at sunset seven days after the first quarter moon and will shed its light through the night.

◆ The third or last quarter (waning) moon always rises about midnight in the eastern sky seven days after the full moon and appears as a half-moon.

◆ The waxing or increasing moon is known and easily remembered as the "right-hand moon." The curve of the right-hand index finger and thumb follows the curve of the increasing crescent. In a similar fashion the waning or decreasing moon can be remembered as the "left-hand moon."

◆ To establish the time of moonrise for each day of the month you add fifty minutes for each day after the beginning of a phase or subtract that amount for each day prior to the beginning of a new phase.

LUCK AND WEATHER

◆ Clear moon, frost soon.

◆ To sweep the house in the dark of the moon will rid it of both moths and spiders.

◆ If Christmas comes during a waxing moon we will have a very good year. The nearer Christmas comes to the new moon the better the next year will be.

◆ If Christmas comes during a waning moon we will have a hard year and the nearer the end of the waning moon so much worse the next year will be.

◆ When the new moon falls on Saturday the following twenty-one days will be wet and windy in nine times out of ten.

◆ When the new moon falls on Monday or "moon-day" it is thought everywhere to be a sign of good luck and good weather.

◆ Two full moons in one calendar month brings good luck.

◆ If the moon changes on Sunday there will be a flood before the month is over.

◆ The nearer the moon's phase change is to midnight the fairer the weather will be for the next seven days. The nearer the moon's change is to noontime the more changeable the weather will be for the following seven days.

◆ A wish on a new moon is a wish come true, if you do not tell your wish and if you kiss the person nearest you.

◆ Thunder coming at the moon's change in the spring often means that the weather will be mild and moist and good crops will follow.

◆ It has been predicted that if the full moon and equinox meet, violent storms will occur followed by a dry spring.

◆ To point to the new moon brings bad luck.

◆ A halo around the moon means rain. If there are stars in the halo it will rain as many days as there are stars, or rain will come after that many days. Five stars or more in the ring means cold weather; fewer stars means warm weather.

- Medicines and tonics are more effective when given at the full moon.

- The new moon is the most powerful phase of the waxing or increasing moon as it has full growth ahead.

MARRIAGE AND BABIES

- Marriage should be performed on a growing moon and the full moon is best.

- Children and animals that are born in the full moon are larger and stronger than those born in the wane of the moon.

- When a boy baby is born in the wane of the moon the next child will be a girl and vice versa.

- When a birth takes place on the growing or waxing moon the next child will be of the same sex.

- Wean boy babies on the waxing or growing moon, but wean girl babies on the waning or decreasing moon. This will make sturdy boys and slim, delicate girls.

MOON MONTHS

From folklore we have received these names:

January	Winter Moon
February	Trapper's Moon
March	Fish Moon or Fisherman's Moon

April	Easter Moon or Planter's Moon
May	Mother's Moon or Spring Moon
June	Stockman's Moon or Mid-Year Moon
July	Summer Moon
August	Dog Days' Moon or Woodcutter's Moon
September	Fall Moon
October	Harvest Moon
November	Hunter's Moon
December	Christ's Moon or Christmas Moon

PLANTING BY THE MOON

> Neither sowing, planting, or grafting should
> ever be undertaken without scrupulous attention
> to the increase or waning of the moon.
>
> —SIR EDWARD TYLOR in *Primitive Culture,* 1871

When the moon is in the phases and signs called "fruitful" it has been established and proven by many that seeds planted at this time germinate in a higher percentage, grow more, thrive better, and produce with more abundance and quality than seeds planted in the "barren" phases and signs.

The old rule used for years was to plant in the new moon period and in a fruitful zodiac sign anything that grows *above* the ground, and in an old moon period with a fruitful zodiac sign anything that produces *underground*. We should, however, be more specific in our planting to properly follow the rhythm

39

and harmony of nature. We should plant in the proper season with the moon's signs and the moon's phases in mind.

As an example: When it is the proper *season* of the year to plant and we are in a "watery and fruitful" *sign* such as Cancer and when the moon is in the *phase* of the first or second quarter, it would be an excellent time to plant any vegetation that is of a juicy, moist, and watery type.

Occasionally it is good to prove the influence of the moon signs. This is best done by planting a portion of your seed in a fruitful sign such as Cancer (June 1 to July 23), and plant more of your seed in Leo (July 23 to August 23), which is the most barren sign. You can do this with only a day or two between plantings as these are adjoining signs. Watch and record the results of plant growth and yield. You may be impressed by the better germination of the seed, growth of the plants, and the amount of yield under these two different signs but also you probably will notice a significant difference in the quality and flavor of the produce.

Planting in the proper season, sign, and phase must of course be accompanied by good agricultural practices. Fertility, soil, moisture, insect control, and other contributing factors must always be considered. Patience, practice, and perseverance in using nature's rules will pay off in better crops and better yields.

THE SIGNS OF THE ZODIAC

The twelve signs of the zodiac each have certain characteristics, elements and tendencies that have a specific influence on all growing things. The zodiac signs through which the moon passes are used as a guide to planting, harvesting, breeding livestock, butchering, and practically all other chores.

The moon makes a complete circle of the earth in about twenty-nine and a half days. The path the moon follows in this monthly voyage is divided into twelve equal parts of 30 degrees each. The separate divisions of this path are called the "Twelve Signs of the Zodiac." Each sign received its name from the constellation of stars contained in it. With the exception of Libra, all the constellations were named after living creatures; "zodiac" means "circle of animals."

The twelve signs are: Aries the ram, Taurus the bull, Gemini the twins, Cancer the crab, Leo the lion, Virgo the virgin, Libra the balance, Scorpio the scorpion, Sagittarius the bowman, Capricorn the goat, Aquarius the waterman, and Pisces the fishes.

The symbols that represent these various signs are usually pictures of the objects they represent. The twelve signs are also identified with the various parts of the human body as early astronomers believed that there was a definite relationship between the heavenly bodies and the earthly body.

The zodiac signs given in most good almanacs today relate to the moon's path around the earth. A few give the signs in relation to constellations of stars which is confusing. The proper zodiac for working with the signs is the moon zodiac.

The calendar year is also divided into the twelve zodiac signs. Moon sign followers use this broad area for determining when to do certain general chores.

When they are pinpointing times to do specific activities such as planting, fishing, or hunting, they want to know the moon sign for that particular day. For this they must know the "moon's place."

41

These are the twelve basic signs of the zodiac covering the cycle of one calendar year:

Sign	Dates	Nature and Character	Governs Body Zones	Planetary Rulers
AQUARIUS	Jan. 20 to Feb. 18	Fixed, airy, barren, dry, masculine	Ankles, legs, body fluids,	Uranus
PISCES	Feb. 18 to March 21	Flexible, fruitful, watery, feminine	Feet	Neptune
ARIES	Mar. 21 to April 20	Movable, fiery, barren, dry, masculine	Head, face	Mars
TAURUS	April 20 to May 21	Fixed, semi-fruitful, productive, earthy, moist, feminine	Throat, neck	Venus
GEMINI	May 21 to June 21	Flexible, fiery, barren, dry, masculine	Hands, arms, chest, shoulders, lungs, nervous system	Mercury

Sign	Dates	Nature and Character	Governs Body Zones	Planetary Rulers
ᴀNCER	June 21 to July 23	Movable, most fruitful, watery, feminine	Breast, stomach	Moon
ᴇO	July 23 to Aug. 23	Fixed, fiery, most barren, dry, masculine	Heart, sides, upper back	Sun
ᴠRGO	Aug. 23 to Sept. 22	Flexible, earthy, barren, moist, feminine	Bowels, solar-plexus	Mercury
ᴠBRA	Sept. 22 to Oct. 23	Movable, semi-fruitful, airy, moist, masculine	Kidneys, loins, lower back, ovaries	Venus
ᴄORPIO	Oct. 23 to Nov. 22	Fixed, very fruitful, watery, feminine	Sex organs, bladder	Pluto
ᴀGITTARIUS	Nov. 22 to Dec. 22	Flexible, fiery, barren, dry, masculine	Hips, thighs, liver, blood	Jupiter
ᴀPRICORN	Dec. 22 to Jan. 20	Movable, productive, earthy, moist, feminine	Knees	Saturn

Most almanacs carry a column called "moon's place." This specifies the zodiac sign that influences each specific day of the month. Every two or three days the moon's place is considered to be ruled by a different zodiac sign. Many farmers heed this daily position of the moon. For example, if the moon's place on a specific day is in a fruitful sign even though the general monthly period is in a dry and barren sign, then the barren period may be overruled on that particular day by the strength of the moon's place daily sign.

DAILY MOON SIGNS

The zodiac signs not only change on the cycle of twelve changes each calendar year but there are also intraweek changes of the signs, called "daily moon signs." These are the signs we must consider in our day-to-day activities. The following is an example of how these weekly changes occur over a one-month period:

TIME AND DATE WHEN LUNA (THE MOON) ENTERS EACH SIGN

	Date	Sign	Time	Phase
1	Mon.	in Aquarius	all day	
2	Tues.	in Aquarius	all day, until	
3	Wed.	enters Pisces	at 11:12 A.M.	
4	Thurs.	in Pisces	all day	
5	Fri.	in Pisces	all day, until	
6	Sat.	enters Aries	at 0:12 A.M.	

(First quarter begins on 7th, at 1:18 P.M.)   Moon on Increase

44

Date		Sign	Time	Phase
7	Sun.	in Aries	all day, until	
8	Mon.	enters Taurus	at 0:40 P.M.	
9	Tues.	in Taurus	all day, until	
10	Wed.	enters Gemini	at 11:35 P.M.	
11	Thurs.	in Gemini	all day	
12	Fri.	in Gemini	all day, until	
13	Sat.	enters Cancer	at 8:18 A.M.	
14	Sun.	in Cancer	all day, until	

(Second quarter begins on 15th, at 5:40 A.M.)		Moon on Increase

Date		Sign	Time	Phase
15	Mon.	enters Leo	at 1:42 P.M.	
16	Tues.	in Leo	all day, until	
17	Wed.	enters Virgo	at 4:32 P.M.	
18	Thurs.	in Virgo	all day, until	
19	Fri.	enters Libra	at 5:32 P.M.	
20	Sat.	in Libra	all day, until	

(Third quarter begins on 21st, at 8:38 P.M.)		Moon on Decrease

Date		Sign	Time	Phase
21	Sun.	enters Scorpio	at 5:38 P.M.	
22	Mon.	in Scorpio	all day, until	
23	Tues.	enters Sagittarius	at 6:50 P.M.	
24	Wed.	in Sagittarius	all day, until	
25	Thurs.	enters Capricorn	at 10:49 P.M.	
26	Fri.	in Capricorn	all day	
27	Sat.	in Capricorn	all day, until	

(Fourth quarter begins on 28th, at 11:47 P.M.)		Moon on Decrease

45

Date	Sign	Time	Phase
28 Sun.	enters Aquarius	at 6:48 A.M.	
29 Mon.	in Aquarius	all day, until	
30 Tues.	enters Pisces	at 5:55 P.M.	

The above is only an example and is not to be followed. Charts of this type which show exactly where the moon is every day of the year, its phase, and its time of entry into the next sign may be obtained from various almanacs.

GENERAL GUIDE TO PLANTING BY THE MOON'S SIGNS

When the moon is in:

Aquarius   A dry, barren sign. Not good for planting. Cultivate, turn sod, destroy pests and unwanted growths.

Pisces   Third in the line of most productive signs, exceeded only by Cancer and Scorpio. Fruitful and productive. A good time to plant when interested in exceptional root growth.

Aries   A dry, barren sign. Not good for general planting, but good for planting onions and garlic. Cultivate, turn sod, dig weeds, destroy noxious growths and pests.

Taurus   A semi-fruitful and fairly productive sign. Has an earthy nature. Excellent for planting potatoes and root crops for quick growth, good for leafy vegetables.

Gemini   A dry, barren sign. Not good for any planting or transplanting. Cultivate, turn sod, destroy pests, weeds, and noxious growths.

Cancer   The most fruitful of all signs. Best sign for planting, transplanting, grafting, budding. Any kind of reliable seed or plants should produce and yield well when started in this sign.

Leo   The most barren zodiac sign. Do no planting. Cultivate and destroy only.

Virgo   Moist but next to Leo in barrenness. Do not plant or transplant. Good for cultivating and destroying.

Libra   A semi-fruitful, moist sign. Very good for pulp and root growth. Plant flowers, root crops, vines, hay, lettuce, cabbage, and corn or hybrids for fodder.

Scorpio Second in line of most productive signs, exceeded only by Cancer. Good for vine growth and strength. Excellent for any planting, transplanting, budding, etc.

Sagittarius Has a barren trend. Good for cultivation and turning sod. Also considered good for seeding hay crops and planting onions.

Capricorn Productive, earthy, and moist. Good for planting root crops, tubers, potatoes, etc. Similar in nature to Taurus but a little dryer.

Do you notice how the signs change from barren to fruitful and back again? Nothing stays the same in nature. Change is ever with us. Nothing is always good; nothing is always bad. We can work with these changes and they will work for us.

> Nothing that is can pause or stay
> The moon will wax the moon will wane
> The mist and cloud will turn to rain
> The rain to mist and cloud again,
> Tomorrow be today.

> —KERAMOS

PLANTING BY THE MOON'S PHASES

In addition to the twelve signs of the zodiac, attention should also be given to the quarters or four phases of the moon. The moon's first and second quarters are called "increasing phases." At this time the moon is steadily growing in size. Plants that produce their fruits above the ground are planted during these two phases. The third quarter is called a "decreasing phase," sometimes referred to as the "dark of the moon." Crops that yield their fruits underground are planted during this quarter. The fourth quarter of the moon, also a decreasing phase, is the best for turning sod, cultivating, and for ridding areas of weeds and noxious growths.

During the first and second quarters the moon is in *increasing* light. Always plant vegetation that yields its produce *above* the ground during this phase. This is particularly true in the case of "annuals," which are those plants that do not continue life from one growing season to the next but must be seeded each year.

First Quarter (new moon, waxing, and *increasing* crescent)

Plant leafy annuals that yield above the ground and have visible outside seed.

EXAMPLES: asparagus, broccoli, Brussels sprouts, cabbage, cauliflower, cereals (corn, barley, oats, rye, wheat), celery, leek, lettuce, parsley, spinach.

Second Quarter (half-moon, first quarter moon, waxing gibbous, and *increasing* light)

Plant leafy annuals that yield above the ground and usually contain seed within their yield.

EXAMPLES: beans, cereals (corn, barley, oats, rye, wheat), cantaloupe, cucumbers, eggplant, muskmelon, peas, peppers, pumpkins, squash, tomatoes, and watermelons.

This is a very fruitful phase and is also good for planting flowers. Many plants do well planted in either of these quarters as they are both "growing phases" for vegetation. For best results plant when the moon is in the most fruitful zodiac *day signs* of Cancer, Scorpio, and Pisces. The semi-fruitful day signs of Taurus, Capricorn, and Libra can also be used as second best. Avoid planting any of the above type plants in the other six zodiac signs.

Third Quarter (full moon, waning gibbous, and *decreasing* light)

Plant bulb and root crops, also biennials and perennials. Plant vegetation that produces its yield *in* the ground.

EXAMPLE: beets, carrots, chicory, garlic, onions, parsnips, peanuts, potatoes, radishes, rhubarb, rutabagas, strawberries, turnips, winter wheat, also any tubers for seed crops. Plant berries, grapes, shrubs, and trees.

Fourth Quarter (last quarter, old moon, dark of the moon, last half-moon, waning crescent, *decreasing* light)

No planting is recommended but if you must plant pick a fruitful zodiac day sign. This is the best period to turn sod, cultivate, pull weeds, destroy noxious growths, and rid areas of pests. Do this especially when the moon is in the barren signs of Leo, Virgo, and Gemini and the barren trend signs of Aries, Aquarius, and Sagittarius.

49

PLANTING TIME VS. GERMINATION TIME

When planting by the signs there is a question as to which time to count, from the time you plant the seed or the time the seed germinates or sprouts.

The time of germination with different bulbs and seeds often varies by several days. The type and nature of the plant, the moisture, the soil, and the temperature have a definite bearing on the time of germination. Beets require seven to ten days; carrots twelve to eighteen; celery ten to twenty; peppers nine to fifteen; radishes three to six; and turnips four to eight days. Since there is such a variation in germination times for different seeds and so many other factors to be considered, it would be very difficult and would require complicated charts to compute times from germination.

Thus remember, when planting by the signs, the time always starts when you put the seed into the earth.

A SUMMARY

Use logic and some "horse sense" when planting by the signs. Plant when the moisture, season, soil, temperature, weather, and any other influencing factors are right. The signs and phases are to be used along with and not in opposition to general conditions. The secret is to try to get as many of these things going for you at one time as you possibly can. The more you have in line, working for you, the better are your chances for outstanding results.

Through trial and error, many attempts, and much experimentation, most folks who "plant by the signs" or do any other activity by the signs, use both the moon's *phase* (quarter) and the moon's daily zodiac *sign* in determining when to act. Just as the moon is in a phase at all times, it is also in a specific zodiac sign every day of the year. If we plan our work by using only the *phase* of moon we may be working during a barren zodiac *sign* and the results will not be good. The two must work hand-in-hand. Knowing where the moon is placed in both phase and sign on each day will help you determine what to do and when to do it—in harmony and rhythm with nature.

We would recommend the use of an accurate almanac in determining the moon's place and the signs of the zodiac for planting and for doing any other activity by the signs. Many almanacs express the daily position of the moon in relation to star constellations. This is incorrect for planting, working livestock, and other activities by about one day. Some people say they have tried planting by the moon signs and it didn't work. They probably missed the fruitful day sign and were in a barren period. Calculations must be made to show the moon's position in the earth's zodiac, not its position in the star constellations. The moon has to be in a fruitful sign of the earth's zodiac for complete success.

THE HARVEST

> If the moon shows like a silver shield,
> You need not be afraid to reap your field,
> But if she rises haloed-round,
> Soon we will tread on deluged ground.
>
> —Traditional

The decay of the old customs of country living and farming are most noticeable in respect to the gathering of the increase. The completion of the growing of crops was a time of joy and celebration. Neighbors would flock together to perform the necessary chores, tables would be set for feasts of mammoth proportions, the air would be filled with laughter and song. Evenings were taken with dancing to the music of an old fiddle in the crisp autumn air under a harvest moon.

Lately, farming has become an industry. There no longer exists the real satisfaction and pleasure of harvest that folks knew in bygone years. With families moving from the farm, the loss of farm labor and the introduction of machinery to do such a large part of the harvesting, the social enjoyment of this part of rural life is past in most communities. Yet there is still a great sense of personal enjoyment and satisfaction when people produce their own crops and livestock and feel the pride of production and a job well done.

HARVESTING BY THE MOON SIGNS

- ◆ All harvesting should be done in a dry moon sign for both easier gathering and better preservation of the crop. The dry zodiac signs to use are Aquarius, Aries, Gemini, Leo, and Sagittarius.

- ◆ The best moon phases to follow in harvesting are the decreasing moons of the third and fourth quarters.

- ◆ Pick apples, peaches, pears, and other fruits when the moon is in decreasing light of the third and fourth quarters. If they are harvested in the increasing moon phases they bruise easily and these spots will rot.

Here are some of the best ways to have good fresh vegetables all through the winter months:

Tomatoes—This is one of the few and perhaps the only vegetable that needs to be canned in order to have a good supply through the cold months. They should be canned for whole tomatoes and for juice.

Carrots—These golden tubers can be stored right in the ground where they grow unless the season turns out to be a very wet one. Cover the whole carrot patch with hay or leaves to prevent freezing. You can then harvest them as you have need. If you have a wet winter, just pull the whole crop and tuck them away in boxes of dry sand in a root cellar.

Potatoes—Sweet potatoes will need to be harvested about the time of frost. Store them in a dry place that has a temperature of about 50–55 degrees F. Irish potatoes can stay in the ground until just before the bone-rattlin' freeze. Then dig them and store in a dark spot at about 40 degrees F. Pick a spot that has good air circulation as these white potatoes are sometimes a little hard to keep.

Squash—The winter variety will keep a few months if you will gather just before the frost and leave a short length of stem on each squash. Store at about 40 degrees F. in a dry place.

Turnips and rutabagas—These can be covered with hay or leaves as carrots and you can eat them through the early winter months. They will keep for a while in a dry, dark root cellar at about 40 degrees F.

53

Cabbage—Bury the heads upside down in dry sand, they will keep a month or two after the bad weather really begins.

Onions—Harvest before the freeze. Store in a cool, dry, dark place and you will have good, sweet onions all winter.

Endive and kale—These can stand until the temperature gets to 15–20 degrees F. right in the garden with a little protection from blasts of cold wind.

Beans and peas—Some folks like to can these when they are at the peak of freshness during the summer and fall months. They can be dried and stored in a cool, dry place.

Broccoli, Brussels sprouts, and kohlrabi—All can take a lot of cold winter weather. Best to just leave them in the garden and eat them as long as they last.

Parsnips—This can be your fresh winter vegetable when most others fail. You can pick them right out of the garden in January, February, and March.

There are others that are special to your locality that offer good eating during the long, dreary winter days. You will need to talk to some of the old-timers in your neighborhood to find out which are best to plant, when to harvest, and how to store them.

MOON SIGNS FOR FARM AND HOME ACTIVITIES

♦ *Cement*—Make and pour cement during the fixed signs of Aquarius, Taurus, Leo, or Scorpio and the cement will "set" better. Also observe the third and fourth quarter moon for this.

◆ *Construction*—Foundations should be dug on fixed signs of Aquarius, Taurus, Leo, and Scorpio in the moon's third and fourth quarters.

◆ *Cultivation and sod turning*—Always do these tasks when the moon is in the barren signs of Aries, Gemini, Leo, Virgo, Sagittarius, or Aquarius. It is best if the moon is in a decreasing light phase such as the fourth quarter.

◆ *Dehydrating or drying*—These chores should be done immediately following a full moon in a dry and fiery sign such as Aries, Leo, or Sagittarius.

◆ *Fencing*—Fence posts will not "heave out" of the ground if set on fixed signs of Aquarius, Taurus, Leo, or Scorpio, and the fourth moon quarter.

◆ *Fertilizing*—The moon should be in a fruitful sign as Taurus, Cancer, Libra, Scorpio, Capricorn, or Pisces. Moon in decreasing light phase, third or fourth quarter.

◆ *Flowers*—Plant in fruitful signs and with moon in increasing light phase, first quarter best. For abundant flowers plant in Cancer, Scorpio, or Pisces; for beautiful flowers and fragrance plant in Libra; for sturdy flowers plant in Scorpio; for hardy flowers plant in Taurus.

◆ *Haircuts*—For faster growth the moon should be in a daily zodiac sign of Pisces, Cancer, or Scorpio which are watery signs, and in an increasing moon phase. For slow hair growth, cut the hair in the daily zodiac sign of Leo, Virgo, or Gemini in the third or fourth moon quarter.

◆ *Irrigation*—For best advantage of water, irrigate when the moon is in a watery day sign, and in the increasing light of the first and second phase.

- *Mowing*—If you wish the grass to come back quickly with increased growth, mowing should be done in the moon's first and second quarter. To retard the growth, mow in the third and fourth quarter on a barren day sign.

- *Painting*—The best time for applying paint is in the decreasing light of the third and fourth quarters of the moon in the fixed signs of Aquarius, Taurus, Leo, and especially Scorpio. Edgar Delaney in Colorado says he will never paint during the watery sign of Cancer in late June. He says the paint will not dry properly, won't make a good finish, and has a tendency to peel.

- *Pruning*—Scorpio is by far the best sign for pruning to limit branch growth and to make better fruit. Should be done with moon in decreasing light phase, third and fourth quarters.

- *Roofing and shingling*—The third and fourth quarters, or the decreasing moon, should be used in the fixed signs of Aquarius, Taurus, Leo, and Scorpio. Work of this type done during the first and second quarters is apt to cause the shingles to buckle and warp. Shingles laid in the waxing moon will swell as the moon grows.

- *Spraying*—Destroy unwanted growths and pests in a barren sign during the decreasing light phase of moon's fourth quarter.

- *Transplanting*—Same as planting; under fruitful signs with moon in increasing light phase of first or second quarter.

Chapter 3

TREES AND THE SIGNS

What a great thought of God was that
when He thought of a tree!

—JOHN RUSKIN, 1890

Farmers of a generation or two ago lived much closer to nature than we do and were aware, or more aware, of trees as indicators of the changing of the seasons. They gauged their planting activities by what the trees told them. Farmers trying to get an early crop of corn didn't want it to be ruined by a slight, late frost. Seth Mowery of Ohio says he planted his entire corn crop by what he read from the hickory buds. Hickory trees have a habit of developing buds slowly no matter how enticing the weather of early spring. They are not often fooled, according to Seth, when nature "runs a little dab of winter back on us." For generations the saying has been: "Plant your corn when the hickory buds are as big as a crow's beak." (Most farmers know about crows, and the size of a crow's beak, since they have chased enough of the pesky rascals out of their fields.) The farmers who have patiently waited for the hickory buds to reach about one inch in length, give or take a little, usually will be the ones with the best and earliest crop.

T. P. Clements used to say "it's corn plantin' time when oak leaves are the size of a nickel and the zodiac signs are in the feet, that makes the stalk take a firm grip in the ground."

CUTTING TIMBER BY THE MOON

The phase of the moon, if waxing or waning, is considered to be of great importance in the felling of timber. This moon sign goes back to the days of Caesar. In those days the very best time to fell trees was when the moon was in conjunction with the sun. The name of this day is "interlinium," sometimes referred to as the "moon's silence."

Cato in *De Re Rustica* instructs on the cutting of timber as follows: "When you root up the elm, the pine, the nut tree, or indeed any other kind of tree, mind and do so when the moon is on the wane, after midday, and when there is no south wind blowing. The proper time for cutting a tree is when the seed is ripe, but be careful not to draw it away or plane it when the dew is falling. Never touch the timber except when the moon is on the change, or else at the end of the second quarter; at these periods you may either root up the tree or fell it as it stands. The next seven days after the full moon are the best of all for grubbing up a tree. Be particularly careful not to rough-hew timber, or indeed, to cut or touch it unless it is perfectly dry; and by no means while it is covered with frost or dew."

Many old-time woodsmen of this country have believed in cutting timber only during the waning of the moon. The belief is that as the moon waned the sap in the timber decreased or moved downward. The wood was then dryer and much easier to cut. They believe the moon has an effect on trees in much the same way as it affects the seas and oceans.

Early-day carpenters would not use wood that had been cut during the waxing moon, saying the wood was full of moisture and would warp, shrink, and was generally unsuitable for construction purposes. Across the country the general rules for cutting timber or wood to give it the greatest durability are:

- Cut chestnut, oak, and other hard woods in the month of August, before noon, after the full moon in the waning quarters.
- Cut pine, maple, and white woods in August, before noon, between the new moon and the full moon phases, in the sign of Virgo.

GRAFTING AND PRUNING BY THE SIGNS

Claude Johnson of Arkansas grafted and budded trees to obtain better varieties of fruit. When he did this work he always used an increasing moon in a fruitful sign. He cut his grafts from good bearing, "never shy" trees during the time the trees were dormant, usually from December through February. The cuttings would be kept in a cool, dark place, preferably with some humidity. He did not want the cuttings to get too dry or too damp while waiting for the right time to make the graft. Grafting would be done just before the sap began to flow. It was always done while the moon was from new to full between the first and second quarters. He would choose, if possible, to do the full job during these increasing phases when the moon was in Cancer—the most fruitful, movable, watery, and feminine of signs. The next best signs were Scorpio, which was a highly rated second, Pisces, for its fruitfulness and good rooting characteristics, and Capricorn, for its productive and earthy nature.

To produce better fruit he would carefully prune his trees. By controlling limb growth in this way he could divert the sap to the primary branches of the tree instead of allowing it to dissipate into greatly spreading and unnecessary branches. The time chosen for this farm chore was usually, but not always, during the trees' dormant months while the sap was down. His pruning was always done during *fruitful* signs in a *decreasing* moon phase, usually the fourth quarter.

TREE TALK

"When the sloe tree is as white as a sheet,
  Sow your barley whether it be dry or wet."

"When the oak puts on his gosling gray,
  'Tis time to sow barley night or day."

"When elm leaves are big as a mouse's ear plant kidney beans,
  if to plant them you are willing,
  When elm leaves are big as an ox's eye, you must plant
  kidney beans if you mean to have any."

"You must look for grass on the top of the oak tree."
  (Grass seldom sprouts well before the oak puts forth.)

"When the hawthorn bloom too early shows,
  We shall have still many snows."

"Cover the roots of all Trees that are bared, and with fat and pregnant Earth lay them close and warme. If any Trees grow barre, bore hole in the Roots, and drive pins or hard wedges of Oake wood therein; and that will produce fruitfulnesse."

—Nicholas Breton (1626)

"To make a barren fruit tree bear fruit, bore a half-inch hole into the heart at sunrise, put sulfur in the hole and drive a wooden pin in it."

—W. J. Brazier

Sam Day of Oklahoma says "never plant corn until the apple trees are in bloom."

Apple trees should be planted during Pisces, a watery sign, and the fruit should be harvested in Libra which is also a moist sign. Ralph Gray of the state of Washington says this will produce superior apples. They will be firm when ripe, bright of color, near perfection in shape, and "the best eatin' apple you ever put in your mouth."

Baker Adams of Oregon has felled trees for five decades and he believes that "timber cut when the moon is old don't get worm-eaten, won't warp, rot, or snap in the fire, and will season better than cut any other time." He especially likes to cut in August and always avoids the watery signs.

When trees are pruned during the proper signs the cuts heal quickly, cover with bark smoothly, and do not leave large knobs.

"Lightning will more often strike trees that are 'poor in fat' than 'fat trees.' Poor trees are cottonwood, catalpa, locust, poplars, and willows. Fat trees are bass, beech, butternut, chestnut, oak and maple."

—Thomas Parrish

61

Chapter 4

BIRDS, POULTRY, AND LIVESTOCK

The first written record we have concerning winged creatures and signs comes from the Bible. Many an old-time country preacher has taken his text for a brush arbor meeting from the story in Genesis about Noah, the ark, and the birds:

"And it came to pass at the end of forty days, that Noah opened the window of the ark which he had made: And he sent forth a raven, which went forth to and fro, until the waters were dried up from off the earth. Also he sent forth a dove from him, to see if the waters were abated from the face of the ground; But the dove found no rest for the sole of her foot, and she returned unto him into the ark, for the waters were on the face of the whole earth: then he put forth his hand, and took her, and pulled her in unto him into the ark. And he stayed

63

yet other seven days; and again he sent forth the dove out of
the ark; And the dove came in to him in the evening; and, lo,
in her mouth *was* an olive leaf pluckt off: so Noah knew that the
waters were abated from the earth. And he stayed yet other seven
days; and sent forth the dove; which returned not again unto
him any more."

—Genesis 8:6–12

Since Noah first used the dove for a sign of dry land, country
people have long worked the land by using the signs given by
birds.

BIRDS AND THE SEASONS

In early rural America birds were often depended upon to
forecast weather for a whole season. Some country folks believed,
and some still do, that "a dry summer will follow when birds
build their nests in exposed places," or "if birds in autumn grow
tame, the winter will be cold for game." Many feel that an unusually early arrival of birds which migrate from the north indicates a severely cold winter will follow. This is backed by the
beliefs of some northwestern residents, and Helmer Harper of
Minnesota who tells us that when birds leave Lake Superior
earlier than usual, fly south fast with few delays en route, and do
not linger at their usual resting places, a hard winter is on its
way.

As a general rule, the arrival of these migratory birds from
Canada will be at about the same time every year. On occasion
some of these birds from the extreme northern areas of the

Arctic Circle are forced to leave those frigid areas when cold rains, snow, and ice destroy the insects on which they feed, cover the vegetation, and freeze the streams. When this happens these birds will come south in rapidly moving large groups. They often bring with them other birds that ordinarily do not come as far south such as crossbills, finches, grosbeaks, and snowbirds. When these latter birds come farther south than usual it is an indication that excessive cold is working in the far northern regions and will almost always move down from Canada and into the northern United States. Sometimes this Arctic blast will have enough force to wash over into the most southern states.

The behavior of these migratory birds is a good weather indicator that the winter will be severe in the far north and that it may come our way.

BIRDS AND WIND

◆ Folks who live in coastal regions say that birds always announce the approach of windy weather. Magpies do their loudest chattering just before a strong wind. Swallows go toward trees, pigeons race after one another with a fierce beating of their wings, sea birds fly inland in groups, and sea gulls gather on land as a sign of an approaching hurricane or bad weather.

◆ If there is any breeze on the beach, gulls and terns can be relied upon to give the direction of the wind. They always rest facing the oncoming wind. This allows them to have unruffled feathers and prepares them for immediate take-off.

POULTRY PROVERBS

There are many old weather proverbs that speak of "signs" given us by the various unusual actions of poultry. Crowing at unusual times, violent and sudden clapping of wings, nervousness in the flock, rolling in the dirt, a crowding together, frantic scratching in search of food, and any other unusual activities and movements are all good indicators. Barnyard fowls and wild birds become nervous and very noisy before there is a drastic and unfavorable change in the weather. Country weather forecasters would say: "When the peacock loudly bawls, we'll soon have both rain and squalls."

We cannot ignore the warnings that poultry and birds tell us about weather and its changes. Their instinct is quite often ahead of any of man's instruments for recording weather changes. Perhaps they can feel the electrical change in the atmosphere that precedes a storm. Though we do not yet know what devices they have as alarms to change, we do know they have them.

USING THE SIGNS WITH BIRDS AND POULTRY

Robert Swenson of Minnesota always tries to set eggs so the hatch will come under the sign of Cancer (June 21 to July 22). This is a fruitful sign and he believes the pullets will mature much more rapidly than those hatched under other signs and will be better layers. If at all possible he tries to have them hatch under the first quarter moon, early in the sign of Cancer.

To follow the signs in hatching birds and poultry you should observe the following:

Select good quality, healthy birds for breeding; know the incubation period of the type birds you are hatching; use the incubation table to select a *day of hatch* when the moon is increasing and in a fruitful sign. The sign of Cancer is best, followed by Scorpio or Pisces. Chicks hatched under the proper sign will be rapid in their maturity, thrifty, and make excellent layers. Birds and chicks hatched during the decreasing moon phases and in a barren sign will not be nearly as good. This has been proven by many good poultrymen. Sid Greenway of Rhode Island says, "Chicks hatched under the right signs are twice as good and worth twice the money as those not incubated with the signs in mind."

Instruct your hatcheryman to have *your* eggs set so they will hatch off on an increasing moon and on a fruitful day. Use this incubation table and a good almanac and you can tell him the exact day to set the eggs for you.

Domestic Fowls	Incubation Days
Canary	13–14
Chicken	19–24 (average 21)
Duck	28
Duck (Muscovy)	33–35
Goose	27–33
Guinea	28
Ostrich	42
Pea Hen	28–30
Pheasant	22–24
Pigeon	16–20
Turkey	26–30

RAISING BIRDS FOR SONG AND BEAUTY

The sign of Taurus rules the throat and many bird breeders believe that having birds hatched under this sign produces good singers. Some breeders strive to have birds hatch under the sign of Libra as this sign is noted for beauty, color, form, and grace. Richard Schuman, at one time a highly recognized birdman in Missouri, says, "Use good breeders, choose a fruitful sign with good aspects for mating, and you can considerably improve bird quality."

NATURE'S WARNINGS ABOUT BIRDS AND POULTRY

Nature does a fine job of warning keepers of birds and poultry of coming problems. Observation can prevent serious losses. Always notice the appearance of the birds, as a sick bird will look sick and act sick, most times early enough for you to correct the problem. Any sick bird will lose eye brightness and will have a listless, pale appearance.

Keep your ears open to strange sounds when you are near your birds. Coughs, sneezes, and wheezing are indicators that action must be taken to prevent serious losses. Drop in feed consumption, weight loss, and any change in appearance and action can be an early warning to health problems.

Another warning that nature gives, which is rather interesting but of a less serious character, is that birds tell us when they are receiving insufficient protein in their feed. Protein requirements vary with various strains of birds and poultry, but from 14 to 18 per cent is usually adequate. When protein drops below the necessary amounts the hen will immediately tell the poultryman by laying smaller eggs. Increased protein in the feed will immediately increase egg size.

Yolks of eggs tell a lot about what chickens have been eating. A bright orange yolk (it's loaded with vitamin A) shows the birds have been allowed to range and feed on grass. Light-colored yolks show they have been caged or confined.

BIRDS AND SUPERSTITION

Birds are sometimes regarded as being supernaturally wise and there are many country omens about them, here are but a few.

◆ Old southern plantation workers believed that doves knew before cotton planting time whether the crops would be good or bad. They thought that before the new ground was broken or the "middles were busted out" the dove knew what the crop yield would be for that season. If the dove flew on the right-hand side of the man as he first started plowing there would be a good crop that year. If it flew on the left hand, the crop would be a failure. They also thought that the dove was particularly accurate in predicting the yield of corn, following the same signs.

These same farm workers believed that the direction from which the cry of the first mourning dove of the season came was important. If the sound of the dove came from above the worker, he would prosper. If it came from any other direction, things would probably not go very well that season.

◆ In the New England states it is still considered unlucky if you see two crows flying together on your left.

◆ In the South it is thought that if two quails fly up in front of you when you are on your way to a business transaction it would be well to postpone the business until another day.

◆ If you break up a killdeer's nest, you will soon break an arm or a leg.

◆ In many parts of the country it is considered bad luck for a bird to flutter against a closed window when you are near that window.

◆ If a rooster crows into the open door of a house it foretells that visitors are on the way.

THE CUCKOO

Of all birds in folklore and mythology, the cuckoo is rated as the highest for its possession of great wisdom. The cuckoo's wisdom is thought to surpass that of other birds in that it knows not only present events but also things that are to come.

This is a carryover from the myths of the ancient Hindu and the early Greeks who thought that cuckoos had these supernatural qualities. Many country folks we have talked with still think the cuckoo has them. Daniel Eaton of Pennsylvania says the old-time farmers of his area would do corn planting only when the song of the brown thrasher or cuckoo was first heard in the spring. These early farmers had little knowledge of future weather conditions. Planting and harvesting was done when it seemed to be the right time. The arrival of the first spring birds, whether it was the cuckoo or brown thrasher, was a signal to them that it was time to begin certain planting tasks. Today we use the almanac for our planting dates. To farmers, especially in the old country, the cuckoo has been a reliable omen for weather and crop planting for many centuries.

LIVESTOCK AND THE MOON

The timing of livestock handling chores, according to numbers of zodiac-following ranchers and stockfarmers throughout the country, should be in harmony and rhythm with the moon and its phases.

♦ *Castration, sterilization, and surgery:* Pecos Caldwell of New Mexico, who has had considerable experience in "marking" livestock, says these operations should be performed only when the moon is in the "feet." This is the Pisces zodiac sign during the decrease of the moon in the third and fourth quarters. Many old-time ranchmen would mark their stock only from February 19 to March 21 when the monthly zodiac sign of Pisces was in effect. Others believe you can operate anytime the *daily* moon sign is in Pisces, but never in Virgo, Libra, Scorpio, or Sagittarius as the animal will bleed too much, not heal properly, and might even die. Most agree that the best time to operate is no earlier than twenty-four hours after the full moon has passed, and some stockmen do this work within one week of the new moon, before or after.

◆ *Shearing:* Sheep and goats should be sheared when the moon is increasing for better quality and more quantities of wool and mohair on the next clip.

◆ *Dehorning:* Remove horns at the new moon or one week before or after. Avoid the daily moon signs of Aries and Taurus as the governing body zone is too near the horn area.

◆ *Butchering and slaughtering:* Roger Smith of Kansas has had many years experience in the butchering of large numbers of cattle, hogs, and sheep. He believes that meat "will keep better, have a fine flavor, and be 'fork cuttin' tender' if you slaughter the first three days after a full moon and don't do any killing during the Leo sign."

◆ *Grazing:* If you have a pasture on which you want the grass to grow back quickly and with increased forage, have the livestock on it only during the first and second quarter phases of the moon. Always have the stock off it from the full moon through the third and fourth quarters. It would be well to time this procedure so that the grass can grow without stock on it during one of the fruitful monthly signs of Pisces, Taurus, Cancer (the best), Scorpio, or Capricorn.

BREEDING OF LIVESTOCK

◆ Set breeding dates so that the birth will occur during the *increasing* light of the moon. The new moon and first quarter are believed to be best.

◆ Set the time of birth to occur in both a feminine and fruitful *daily* moon sign. Cancer, Scorpio, or Pisces are best as they are the most feminine, the most fruitful, and are also water signs. Taurus and Capricorn, the semi-fruitful signs, should be avoided as the date of birth.

Chapter 5

COUNTRY COOKING

Country women have always been known for the tasty food they put on the table every day of the year. They are also known for the tempting dishes that they carry to picnics, church, and community suppers and to family reunions.

Some women, and some men, too, are noted for their unusual dishes. We have assembled some of the most unusual old country recipes from our collection. The majority of these recipes have probably never appeared in a published cookbook—they have been written on scraps of paper and handed down from one country cook to another through the years.

If times get tough you might want to try some of these, but even if you never use any of them they still make interesting reading.

CHICKEN SOUP

Put two gallons of water, a slice or two of bacon, and a fat hen in a kettle on the top of the stove. Let it boil until very tender. Remove the fowl, mincing all the white meat and a small portion of the dark. Combine the yolks of two hard-boiled eggs, a tablespoonful of butter, pepper, salt, and celery seed to taste. Mix these ingredients into the meat and return to the pot liquor, at which time it should have boiled down to about two quarts. Stir all together, and as soon as it comes to a boil add one pint of milk and thicken with a teaspoonful of flour. When it comes to a boil remove from the fire, as the milk is apt to curdle if allowed to boil too long. This is a very rich soup.

CALF'S HEAD SOUP

Prepare a calf's head, and take out the brains. Place the head in a kettle. To this add one gallon of water. Boil until it comes to pieces, then take out all the bones. Return the remains to the vessel, adding one tablespoonful of butter, one small teacup of browned flour, one teacup of tomato catsup, one tablespoonful of allspice, and one nutmeg grated. Season with salt and pepper to taste. When soup is nearly ready for the table, fry the brains and add. A few minutes before serving add one teacup of wine, one small teaspoonful of cloves and same of mace. Sliced lemons or hard-boiled eggs are a nice addition.

OX TAIL SOUP

The day before the soup is wanted, take three ox tails, cut them in pieces, and put on to fry in butter, first removing all the fat. Let them brown well, then set aside until the next day. Take off all the grease that may be around them, and put to boil in about three quarts of water; add some salt, pepper and allspice to taste, and from two to four onions, one carrot, one turnip, and one head of celery. Boil four or five hours; lift out the meat; strain; choose some of the best of the meat, return it to the soup, and serve.

RABBIT SOUP

Cut up a pair of rabbits into neat, small pieces; take all the nicest bits and fry them until light brown. Have a pot of stock, and into it put the inferior pieces of the rabbit, two onions, a carrot, a head of celery, some parsley and thyme, a blade of mace, a clove or two, salt, and pepper. Let this all boil until the meat falls off the bones, then pass it through a sieve. Put the soup back into the pot, using some of it to make gravy over the bits of rabbit in the frying pan, then turn the contents of the frying pan into the soup pot, and let it simmer until the meat is tender. Slightly thicken the soup with a little browned flour.

GENUINE TURTLE SOUP

For a turtle weighing thirty to thirty-five pounds, use five pounds of beef, five pounds of veal, and one pound of ham. Butter the bottom of the soup pot and arrange the meat in the pot in layers, with four onions, one carrot, eighteen cloves, one teaspoonful of pepper, and one full pint of water. Put the pot over a brisk fire, stirring frequently until the entire pot is covered with a brown glaze; then fill the pot with the water in which the turtle was boiled (if this does not fill the pot add more water). Put the pot on a low fire, and let it cook very slowly for two hours; skim well, then strain off this pot liquor, adding one quart of water to the meat. Boil it another hour, and then strain into the other pot liquor.

To make the soup, put a half pound of butter into a large soup pot, with a bouquet of the following herbs: five sprigs of savory, five of thyme, four of basil, five of marjoram, and four bay leaves. Place it for a few minutes over a moderate fire; be careful that it does not change color; then stir in very gradually one half of a pound of flour to form a roux, and keep stirring over the fire until it becomes browned lightly. Remove it from the fire and stir now and then until nearly cold, then add the stock, which should be at least six quarts. Place it again over the fire and stir until boiling. It must then simmer two hours. Pass it through a colander into a clean stew pan, add the turtle meat (which has been cut into squares), and place the pan on the fire, where it will simmer until the meat is very tender. Then add the green fat, and salt to taste, and let it stew ten or fifteen minutes longer. When ready to serve add a very small teaspoonful of cayenne pepper, and one-half pint of Madeira wine. Serve on a plate with lemons cut in slices.

MOCK TURTLE SOUP

Take a calf's head and feet with skin on; put into a pot with about a pail of water; add two onions and skim well when boiling. Boil until the meat falls from the bone; then strain, skim again and turn the soup back in the pot. Add full tablespoonfuls of cloves, salt, pepper, mace, nutmeg, and a little red pepper. Cut up half the meat and add to the soup, just heating it through, then set it aside. Next day add more spice and a little butter (with flour rubbed in), one pint of port wine, lemon slices, and sliced hard-boiled eggs.

GUMBO SOUP

Cut up in small pieces four skinned squirrels and one chicken, and boil until the flesh falls from the bones. To each gallon of soup add a handful of green or dried sassafras buds, enclosed in a cheesecloth bag. Add one quart of okra, one large onion cut fine, a half-dozen medium-sized Irish potatoes cut in cubes, one carrot grated, and a small quantity of cabbage. Season with pepper and salt. When the soup is done take the bag out, and, after removing the buds, wring the bag into the soup. Add red pepper and thicken with browned flour.

BOUILLON

In a kettle put two pounds of lean beef, two pounds of veal, and an old chicken hen. Cover well with cold water. Place the soup kettle on the back of the stove where it will boil very slowly; as it does so, the fibers of the meat will enlarge. If cooked too rapidly, the meat hardens so that the water cannot penetrate it. Boil three hours or until the meat is tender, removing every particle of scum as it rises. When thoroughly tender, remove from the fire and let it stand in a cool place all night. Carefully remove every particle of fat from the stock; strain and return to the fire to boil, adding the following vegetables: one head of celery, a sprig of parsley, one turnip, three carrots, two onions, half teaspoonful of peppercorns, four whole cloves, a few tomatoes, and a bunch of sweet herbs. The vegetables must be sliced very thin before adding. Boil about one hour, and just before straining a second time, add salt. The yolks of four eggs well beaten is sufficient for three quarts of bouillon. A few drops of cold water should be added to the egg, pouring upon it the boiling bouillon. Serve in cups.

PEPPER POT

Take fish flesh, and chicken or other fowl, in as nearly equal parts as possible. Add to this one pound of beef or mutton cut in very small pieces. Put into a soup pot; cover with sufficient quantity of water; add a red pepper, boiling all until tender. Skim the liquid, and if not sufficient in quantity, add boiling water. Then add one large onion, sliced. Salt to taste. Add sliced potatoes and small dumplings made of flour and butter. Boil until the ingredients are all tender. Serve hot.

SOUSE CHEESE

Put pork meat in cold water, and let it stand several days, changing the water every day. Scrape well each time the water is changed. If the weather is warm use a little salt in the water. Scraping the meat often will make it white. Boil the meat in sufficient water to cover it; as soon as it is tender drop it in milk-warm water, and when thoroughly cold, in salt water. The hog head should be boiled until the bones are about to leave the meat. Put in a few hog ears scraped very white and boil also. Chop the whole very fine and season to taste with pepper and salt; put the meat in a bowl and place a weight on top. When ready slice and serve with vinegar.

SAUSAGE MEAT

To fifteen pounds of choice lean ground pork, add seven pounds of ground fat, seven tablespoonfuls of salt, seven of sage, two and one half of thyme, six of pepper, and four of sweet marjoram. Mix the meat well with the seasoning; keep in a cool, dry place.

HOW TO CURE PORK

First sprinkle a little salt over the pork, and lay it in a vat four or five days. Then put the pork in a barrel and cover each layer with salt. The barrel must be kept well covered. Next make a brine strong enough to float a potato, and add two hundred pounds of meat and two ounces of saltpetre.

HOW TO KEEP CURED MEATS

Procure a large box, and cover the bottom with a layer of common field corn (shelled). Put in a layer of the meat, another of corn, alternately, in this way until the box is nearly filled, with a thick layer of the corn on top. This is an excellent way to keep hams, shoulders, or side meat. The corn can be used for fattening hogs and other purposes after the meat has all been used. All who try this plan will like it.

THE VIRGINIA WAY OF CURING HAMS

Put a teaspoonful of saltpetre on the fleshy side of each ham, salt not too heavily for five weeks (if the weather is freezing cold, six weeks); then brush the hams well and rub them with hickory ashes. Let them stay for one week, then hang and smoke them for six weeks with green hickory chips. After brushing, pack them in hickory ashes.

HOW TO COOK PIGS' FEET

Clean the feet well and soak until very white. Wrap each foot in a piece of cloth, tying it well with a cord. Boil them three or four hours; let them remain in the cloth until needed. When cooked in this way they will be found very delicate and tender, and are nice for frying, broiling, or pickling.

HOW TO ROAST A GOOSE

Singe, remove the pin feathers of a goose, and before it is cut or drawn, wash and scrub thoroughly in soap suds to open and cleanse the pores and render the oil easily extractable. Then draw, wash and rinse the inside in clear water, and wipe dry. Stuff with mashed potatoes, highly seasoned with onions, sage, salt, and pepper. Sew and truss; put on a rack in a pan and cover the breast with slices of fat and salt pork.

Place it in the oven for three quarters of an hour. The pork fat is quickly drawn out by the heat, flows over the goose, and aids in drawing out the oil. When considerable oil is extracted, take the pan from the oven and pour off all the oil. Remove the pork and dredge the goose with flour, and place again in oven. When the flour is browned, add a little hot water and baste often. Dredge with flour after basting. Cook until brown and tender. Make a gravy. Garnish with watercress and serve with applesauce.

WILD TURKEY

Wash and wipe the turkey very carefully; wipe the cavity with a dry, soft cloth before you stuff. Have a rich forcemeat, bread crumbs, some bits of fat pork chopped fine, pepper, and salt. Moisten with milk, beat in an egg, and add two tablespoonfuls of melted butter; stuff the cavity with this mixture. Baste the turkey with butter and water for the first hour; then three or four times with the gravy; finally, five or six times with melted butter. Dredge with flour at the last; with butter when it is of a nice brown and serve. Skim the gravy, add a little hot water, and pepper; thicken with the giblets chopped fine and browned flour. Boil up and pour into tureen, or put one giblet under each wing when the turkey is dished. Garnish with sliced lemon or parsley—and send around currant jelly or cranberry sauce with it.

PARTRIDGE AND QUAIL

Prepare partridge and quail as you would chickens, but leave the feet on, scalding them and drawing off their skin; skewer up the feet, crossed over the vent, larder the breast with boiled ham fat, roast over a moderate fire forty minutes, and baste with butter before you "take them up." Make a gravy from half a pint of stock (white) and one spoonful of flour and two of butter, braided together, or serve with bread sauce. Garnish with slices of lemon.

BROILED PIGEONS OR SQUABS

Split down the back and broil as you would chickens, seasoning with salt, pepper, and butter. Broil slices of pork and place over each bird and serve.

ROAST PIGEONS

Prepare and roast the same as chickens. Pigeons should be eaten within six hours after being killed, as they lose their flavor if kept too long.

HOW TO STEW PIGEONS

Prepare as for roasting them. Cut strips of salt pork an inch long and half an inch wide, roll the strips in pepper, and place a strip in the body of each bird with a piece of bread of the same size, then fill the bodies with bits of sour apples. Lay the pigeons in a stew pan, breast down, dredge with flour, and pour in just enough water to cover them. Season with salt and pepper, and stew over a moderate fire one hour. Serve in a dish with the gravy.

ROAST DUCKS

Having trussed the ducks, put into each a thick piece of soft bread that has been soaked in port wine. Place over a quick fire and roast from three-quarters to an hour. Make a gravy by slowly stewing the ground giblets of the ducks in butter rolled in flour and as little water as possible. Before sending to the table squeeze over each duck the juice of a lemon or orange, and serve them up very hot with the gravy. Eat them with currant jelly.

HOW TO STEW DUCKS

Place the giblets in a saucepan with the yellow rind of a lemon pared thin, a very little water, a piece of butter rolled in flour, a very little salt, and cayenne. Let them stew gently, keeping the saucepan covered. Half-roast the ducks, saving the gravy that falls from them. Then cut them up, put in a large stew pan with the gravy (having first skimmed off the fat) and just water enough to keep them from burning. Place the pan over a moderate fire and let them stew gently till done. Toward the last (having removed the giblets) pour over the ducks the gravy from the small saucepan, and stir in a large glass of port wine and a glass of currant jelly. Send them to table as hot as possible.

NOTE: Any duck may be cooked as above. The common wild ducks, teal, etc., should always be parboiled with an onion or large carrot in the body, to extract the fishy taste. On tasting you will find the carrot or onion to have imbibed that disagreeable flavor.

Wild ducks should be a little underdone, stuffed with forcemeat and chopped onions, and served with sharp sauce and cole slaw.

SNOW BIRDS

Stuff each bird with an oyster, place in a dish, add a little boiled pork, and oyster liquor, season well with butter, pepper, and salt. Cover the dish with a rich crust and bake in a moderate oven.

GUINEA

Two of these are generally served for a dish, one of which should be larded, and the other covered with a layer of fat bacon. Roast them before a brisk fire for about forty-five minutes; glaze and dish them up with watercress; pour some gravy under them, and serve bread sauce separately.

QUAIL PIE

After the quail have been cleaned, salt and pepper them and stuff with bread crumbs or oyster dressing, and stew a few minutes, keeping them well covered. Cover a dish with rich puff paste, put in your birds, sprinkle in some minced parsley, hardboiled eggs cut up fine, and flakes of butter rolled in flour. Add the gravy in which the birds were stewed, cover with paste, and bake in a moderate oven about one hour. A little lemon juice is an addition to this pie.

A NICE WAY TO COOK GAME BIRDS

Partridge, quail, plover, pheasant, etc. are very nice stuffed with chestnuts—boiled, and mashed or pounded. Cover the birds with thin slices of cold ham; lay in a deep dish, and when done remove the ham and dish the birds, pouring the gravy over them.

BROILED SQUIRREL

Clean well, and put in salted water for at least one hour; then wipe dry. Have a hot fire, heat your gridiron, and broil the squirrel, turning often. When done, place on a platter with melted butter; season with salt and pepper, and garnish with slices of lemon. Serve when first cooked.

SQUIRREL PIE

Carefully skin and clean a pair of squirrels, cut in small pieces, put in a stew pan and cook, adding two slices of salt pork, with sufficient water to stew them until about half done. Season and thicken the gravy. Put into a deep dish, cover with a nice pie crust, and bake in a moderate oven until done.

FRIED RABBIT

Clean and wash well; then boil a few minutes. When cold cut rabbit into joints, dip into beaten egg, then roll in cracker crumbs, seasoned with salt and pepper. Fry in a butter and lard mixture until nicely browned. Remove the pieces of rabbit, thicken the gravy with a little flour, pour in a cup of milk or cream, let it come to a boil, and pour over the rabbits. Serve hot with onion sauce. Garnish with sliced lemon.

STEWED RABBIT

Skin and clean nicely and cut into pieces; put a generous piece of butter into a stew pan and brown the rabbit. Remove the meat, add to the butter one pint of boiling water, one table-spoonful of flour stirred to a paste in cold water, salt to taste, and a little grated onion. Let it boil up and then put in the meat; stew slowly till tender. Serve hot.

ROAST RABBIT

After the rabbit has been thoroughly washed put it in salted water for an hour or more. Stuff with bread crumbs and sausage meat, season well with salt, pepper, and a well-beaten egg, and sew up. Then put in the roasting pan one onion, one carrot cut up, a few cloves, whole peppercorns, and a bay leaf. Rub well with salt and pepper, and lay upon the dressing, putting bits of butter here and there over the rabbit. Sift little flour over the top, pouring in a little hot water. Cover closely and roast, basting very often. When done, place on a hot platter and garnish with wine and slices of lemon.

GROUND HOG

To cook ground hog cut a big onion and place in water used to preboil the meat. Preboil three times, drain off water and onion, roll meat in flour and fry.

VENISON STEAK

Heat the gridiron over a clear, hot fire. Butter the bars before putting on the steaks. Broil rapidly, turning often in order to keep in the juices. Have a warm dish at hand with a spoonful of butter melted to dip your steaks in when done. Salt and pepper and cover to keep warm. Then heat a little claret, add a few spoonfuls of currant jelly to it, and pour over steak just before serving. For fried venison add chopped onions the last few minutes of frying and serve with slices of lemon.

VENISON PIE

Cut the meat into small pieces. Put them into a stew pan with one onion; add salt, pepper, and nutmeg, and just enough cold water to cook until tender. Have ready a good pie crust; roll and line a deep pie plate with this and fill with the meat.

Before putting this in the pie crust, roll some flakes of butter in flour and put over the pie. Cover with a thick layer of pastry, and make a hole in the center of the top crust; bake slowly. Heat some port wine, into which you have thrown some cloves and mace. When the pie is nearly done, pour this mixture into the pie through the hole in the top crust; brush the top with beaten egg; return to the oven and bake until a light brown.

UNCLE ED'S RECIPE FOR COOKING 'POSSUM

"Go out in de woods and catch a nice fat 'possum and take 'im home, put on a pot o' wattah an' heat it jis' like you wus gwine to clean a pig, an when it git hot fling in a shovel o' ashes an' dip 'im in it an' den you scrapes all de ha'r an fur off 'im and fix it jist like a little pig, 'cept you splits 'im open an spreads 'im out flat. Den you hangs 'im in a tree two or three nights an he's reddy fur de oven. When you goes to cook 'im, lay 'im flat on de bottom and fill 'im wid slices o' sweet 'tater and put mo' all round 'is sides. Den you sets 'im over de coles and kivers 'im wid a hot lid and cook's 'im mity slo' till he dun good an tender. De flavor of de 'possum, an it's jis' good 'nuff to make you lick yo' fingers."

DUMPLINGS

1 cooking spoon lard
2 cups flour
2 rounded teaspoons cream of tartar
1 level teaspoon soda
Salt
Milk
1 cup sugar
1 tablespoon butter
1 pint boiling water
Cream (optional)

Work lard into flour which has been mixed and sifted with cream of tartar, soda, and salt. Add sufficient milk to make a soft dough. Roll and cut into squares. Place slices of cooked apples, peaches or pears, or fresh berries on each square. Fold over and pinch edges. Turn upside down in a bread pan, four to a pan. Make a syrup of sugar, butter, and boiling water. Pour syrup over dumplings and bake over a low flame forty-five minutes. Serve with or without cream.

OLD-FASHIONED MINCEMEAT

8 cups chopped apples
1 pound ground pork
1½ cups molasses
1 pint old cider
1 pound raisins
1 pound currants
1 cup sugar
2 pounds suet, chopped fine
1 quart water in which beef is cooked
Salt
¼ pound citron, chopped fine

Mix ingredients, heat gradually, stir occasionally, and cook slowly two hours over a low flame. Add ground spices to taste after mincemeat is cooked or when making pies.

INDIAN PUDDING

1 quart milk
½ cup cornmeal
½ cup molasses
1 teaspoon salt
1 teaspoon ginger or cinnamon
1 cup cold milk
Cream (optional)

Heat the quart of milk and stir in the meal slowly until it thickens. Take from the stove and add molasses, salt and spice. Put mixture into a buttered earthen pudding dish and add cold milk. Bake over a low flame for two hours. After the pudding is partly cooked a little more cold milk may be added if desired. Serve with or without cream.

SUGAR PIES—SOUTHERN STYLE

3 cups light brown sugar
½ cup cream
½ cup melted butter
3 eggs
Lemon

Mix ingredients, beating well. Season with lemon and bake in pastry without a top crust. Use low flame.

COUNTRY COFFEE

Years ago coffee came in what we always called a tow-sack—some folks call it a gunnysack. The coffee beans were green and had to be roasted. Roasting was generally done in a long-handled cast iron frying pan, called a spider in New England, and a skillet in the Southwest. A lid was put on this roasting device and the coffee beans would jump like Mexican jumping beans or popcorn. The trick was to roast the beans without scorching them, so a lot of coffee was made from scorched beans instead of the roasted kind.

Then the famous Arbuckle brothers, Charles and John, came into the picture. They got the money-making idea of roasting the beans themselves on a professional basis and packing them in a handy one-pound sack. Their pack became so·popular that for a long time coffee wasn't called coffee any more in some parts of the country—it was called Arbuckle. A lot of old-timers in the country still call it that.

Arbuckle Brothers coffee, even though roasted, was still in the whole bean form and had to be ground. Coffee grinders were listed in the catalogues and were in almost every general store. Every home had to have one, and it took many a turn of the crank to grind a pound of coffee. Even today the best coffee you can pass over your lips is that made from a freshly ground whole roasted coffee bean. Here are a few more pointers on making really good country coffee:

◆ Use the very best water. Alkali water, high mineral content (hard) water, and deep well water *do not* make the best coffee. Rain water, melted snow water, and sparkling pure mountain spring water make the best coffee by far.

◆ The best coffeepot is one made of cast iron and the gallon size is the best.

◆ Be sure the pot is absolutely clean before making coffee. Modern scouring soaps are not recommended for this cleaning job as they leave a taste that is far worse than the taste of the old coffee.

◆ Fresh mud, wet clay, or caliche mud is the best cleaning agent you can use to scour the inside of a coffeepot. Don't worry too much about the outside as it will get smoke black again anyway.

95

◆ When the pot looks and smells clean, fill it about three-quarters full of good, cold water—never warm water. Fresh grind about a third of a pound of roasted coffee beans. Dump these into the water and set the pot on the fire. Do not cover the pot but keep your eye on it and when the brew begins to bubble then stir it. It will foam at this point so stir until the foaming stops to keep it from boiling over. When the deep boiling sets in move the pot away from the fire but still near enough that the heat of the fire keeps the coffee rolling around the side of the pot. If you keep the coffee plenty hot but just below boiling it will be fine for hours. You can add more water and more fresh ground coffee if needed and it will be good. You must keep the coffee hot, not boiling but very near. If it ever cools it will never be good again and you will need to make a fresh pot. Here is another way good country coffee is made:

◆ To every cup of water add a teaspoon to a tablespoon of ground coffee; then add one for the pot. Put it in cold water and allow to boil just once. Remove from fire. Settle with ¼ cup of cold water and serve piping hot.

◆ Some country folks like it this way: bring water to boil first. Add coffee, boil five minutes, settle, and serve. (You can put your coffee in a small muslin bag tied loose, then boil five minutes longer and your bag of grounds can be removed before serving.)

Sometimes it is necessary to find a substitute for coffee when rations are low. Here are three ways to do it:

◆ Parched barley, beans, rice, and bread crumbs make a fair coffee substitute. Scorch them a bit and grind. An improvised coffee mill can be a bag and a stone, pounding the materials to a fine pulp.

◆ Wash carrots and slice into pieces about half-inch thick. Dry them in the sun or oven but do not cook. When they are dry, brown them well and use as coffee. If you have a little real coffee left to mix with the carrots it makes a fine brew.

◆ Okra seeds should be roasted or browned the same as coffee beans. Alone, they make one of the finest coffee substitutes but if you can add just a little coffee with them it is even better.

MOON SIGNS IN THE KITCHEN

Country women who heed the zodiac signs in their kitchen work agree with these tips:

◆ *Baking:* Bread prepared when the moon is in the first and second, or waxing quarters tends to "rise" more. Baking is best done when the moon is in Aries, Cancer, Libra, or Capricorn, the movable signs. Some believe this makes the bread lighter.

◆ *Brewing and Winemaking:* The third and fourth waning moon quarters are usually best, especially when the moon is in the watery and fruitful signs of Pisces, Cancer, or Scorpio.

◆ *Canning:* Can fruits and vegetables during a waning moon in the third and fourth quarters, preferably in the watery signs of Pisces, Cancer, or Scorpio. Put up jellies and pre-

97

serves during a waning moon in the third and fourth quarters, but in the fixed signs of Aquarius, Taurus, Leo, or Scorpio (especially Scorpio since it is both a fixed and a water sign).

A HASH OF KITCHEN WISDOM

- Molasses and syrup will pour completely out of a cup or any container if you will first grease it with butter or cooking oil.

- When cooking onions set a cup of vinegar on the stove to kill the odor.

- When boiling eggs, add a little salt to the water and the shells will slip off easily. To boil an egg that is cracked, add a teaspoonful of salt to the water and the egg will stay in the shell.

- Roll an orange, grapefruit, or lemon vigorously on a hard surface before squeezing it and you will get a lot more juice.

- A cup of water placed in the oven when you bake will keep the crust of bread and cake from getting hard.

- Odorless cabbage cooking is accomplished by adding half a green bell pepper without seeds to the cabbage pot. It flavors the cabbage and kills the odor in the kitchen.

- To easily slip tomato peels off place the tomatoes in boiling water for one-half minute then place them in cold water until they are cool. The skin will slip off and leave a firm, full, unbroken tomato.

◆ Raw milk curdles quickly when boiled. This can be corrected by adding a pinch of soda.

◆ A pinch of salt in raw milk will keep it from souring quickly.

◆ Sprinkle table salt on scorched milk and it will help eliminate the bad smell.

◆ When cooking with milk, put a little water in the pan first and heat it to boiling, then add the milk. It will keep the milk from burning or sticking to the bottom of the pan.

◆ The taste of oversalted vegetables can be removed by covering the bowl with a wet cloth for a few minutes.

◆ If whipping cream won't whip add the white of an egg.

◆ When cake sticks to the pan, wrap a damp warm cloth around the baking pan. The steam will cause the cake to loosen.

◆ Soak hard-shell nuts in salt water overnight. They will break open easily and the kernels will shell-out whole.

◆ Dip fresh fish in hot salt water until the scales curl and they will be a lot easier to clean.

Chapter 6

RURAL REMEDIES

When the nearest doctor lived many miles away folks were forced to rely on their own knowledge to treat a wide variety of ailments. Most families had a "doctor book" of some fashion, often handwritten, that contained instructions for home treatment. The treatments and medications were handed down from family to family. This important book often took its place beside the family Bible. Ethel Rogers of South Carolina said years ago that "the Bible shows *how* to live and the doctor book shows how to *live*."

Here are some of the choice home remedies from Ethel's "doctor book" and from others over the country (we'd advise caution in applying these).

◆ *Arthritis:* Take a teaspoon of chopped garlic twice a day with water for relief from the pain and swelling of arthritis.

◆ *Bleeding:* Apply a mixture of flour and salt and wrap with cloth or common paper; or press cobwebs and brown sugar over the cut.

◆ *Blisters:* Boil the bark from an oak tree in a small amount of water and apply to blisters.

◆ *Bone felon:* Saturate a piece of turnip in turpentine and apply to the felon.

◆ *Bruises:* Wash with warm water and anoint with tallow or candle grease.

◆ *Burns:* The juice from the succulent plant aloe vera applied often is very good. Apply ice directly to burn.

◆ *Chapped hands and lips:* Apply castor oil or equal parts of glycerine and lemon juice often to area. Ointment used on cows' teats is a fast cure for chapped hands. Rubbing hands regularly in sheep's wool will work too.

◆ *Chills and cramps:* Mix ginger and pepper in very hot water and drink.

◆ *Colds and flu:* Mix and drink a mixture of cinnamon, sage, and bay leaves, and add a little lemon juice. Drink warm. Drink hot ginger tea freely. Take a dose of quinine every six hours. Drink juice of citrus fruits often.

◆ *Constipation:* Eat freely of preserves, drink plenty of water; eat garlic.

◆ *Cough:* Make a tea of wild cherry bark; mix with honey. Take a teaspoonful as needed.

◆ *Cuts and scratches:* Rub with a sliced clove of garlic or apply raw honey.

◆ *Diarrhea:* Brown a little flour over the fire, add two tea-spoonfuls of vinegar and one teaspoonful of salt, mix and drink. Mixing a tablespoonful of warm vinegar and a tea-spoonful of salt will cure most severe cases. Do not eat fruit. A hot drink of ginger tea is often good. Repeat any of the above every few hours. Take sips of water often.

◆ *Earache:* A piece of cotton sprinkled with pepper and moistened with oil or fat will give almost instant relief. Wash with warm water. Place small piece of garlic in ear.

◆ *Frozen ears, fingers, nose, etc.:* Never rub snow on these tender members. Use warmth of hand to rub, thaw, and restore circulation. Dip affected areas in cold water, then add warm water gradually until water reaches blood heat, and massage area.

◆ *Headache:* Inhale fumes of boiling vinegar.

◆ *Hiccups:* Eat a tablespoonful of peanut butter.

◆ *Hives:* Bathe with rubbing alcohol and follow with a strong solution of baking soda and water over the affected area. Do not drink anything cold.

◆ *Inflamed eyes:* Bind on hot tea leaves or raw fresh meat, leave on for several hours then wash well with warm water.

◆ *Insect bites:* Apply common mud, a slice of onion, garlic juice, lemon juice, baking soda, tobacco, or honey.

◆ *Ivy or oak poisoning:* Wash area often with a cooling solution of baking soda and water and apply apple cider vinegar, or squeeze the juice from jimson weed and use as a lotion.

◆ *Liver ailments:* Mix pure olive oil and lemon juice in warm water and drink once each day.

- *Mosquito bites:* Apply ammonia, camphor, tar soap, or crushed pennyroyal weed.

- *Nervousness:* Chew snakeroot or drink a tea made from dandelion leaf, passion flower, plantain leaf, peppermint, snakeroot or valerian.

- *Nervous stomach:* Drink bottled mineral water or make your own mineral water by buying some powdered slaked lime (be sure it is slaked lime) at the drugstore. Add one teaspoonful to one quart water. Shake well. Put in refrigerator and leave until the lime has settled to the bottom of the jar. Pour off the clear, top liquid and drink a few swallows for stomach relief.

- *Poisoning:* Give a strong emetic of warm water, mustard, and salt mixed. Cause vomiting by swallowing small piece of soap or tobacco.

- *Ringworms:* Apply kerosene to area three times each day until ring and redness disappears. Juice from a green walnut hull also drives out ringworm.

- *Scalds:* Relieve instantly by using common baking soda applied thickly to wet rags and placed on scalded area. If baking soda is not available flour may be used.

- *Sleeplessness:* Drink a glass of warm milk; or mix equal parts of apple cider vinegar and honey, take two teaspoonsful each hour.

- *Sore throat:* Apply fat bacon or pork to outside of throat and hold in place by tying a rag around it. Keep in place until soreness is gone. Swab the throat with diluted tincture of iron. Gargle with warm salt water or apple cider vinegar, repeat often. Hold small piece of garlic in mouth for several minutes, several times during the day.

◆ *Spasms of muscles, cramps:* Eat two teaspoons of honey with each meal.

◆ *Speck in eye:* Place flaxseed in eye to absorb particle.

◆ *Sprains:* Mix sea salt and cider vinegar into a paste and apply; or apply epsom salts with a cloth wet in vinegar.

◆ *Sunburn:* Apply butter or buttermilk, boil tan oak or commercial wet ground tea and apply frequently. Wet dressings of epsom salts or baking soda also help.

◆ *Toothache:* Mix warm vinegar and salt, hold in mouth until pain ceases. For cavities, plug with cotton doused with pepper and ginger.

◆ *Warts:* The juice from milkweed or castor oil will take away warts when applied regularly.

MOON SIGN MEDICINE

Followers of moon signs in the treatment of human and animal ailments say that all procedures should be in rhythm with the moon and its various phases. Most agree that proper timing should be as follows:

◆ *Dental work:* Cavities should be filled during a waning moon period of the third and fourth quarter and in a fixed sign of Aquarius, Taurus, Leo, or Scorpio. Teeth should be extracted during a waxing moon period of the first and second quarters, but only in the signs of Pisces, Gemini, Virgo, Sagittarius, or Capricorn. Plates are best made under a decreasing moon of the third and fourth quarters and in a fixed sign of Aquarius, Taurus, Leo, or Scorpio.

◆ *Operations:* The best time to have operations, pull teeth, remove tonsils, or remove any growth is when the signs are in the knees or feet (the best), such as Capricorn or Pisces.

◆ *Removal of noxious growths* (this includes corns, callouses, superfluous hair, warts, any unwanted growths): Use a barren sign such as Aquarius, Aries, Gemini, Leo, Virgo, or Sagittarius with the moon in the fourth quarter.

◆ *Surgical procedures:* Choose a time when the moon is on the increase in the first and second quarters. Vitality and thrifty conditions prevail and wounds tend to heal better and faster during this time. An exception is the cutting away of noxious growths, and this should be done on a decreasing moon, third and fourth quarters.

Do not have an operation during the period the moon is in a ruling sign of that part of the body on which the operation is to be performed. Heart operations, for example, should not be performed during the sign of Leo unless absolutely necessary, as Leo rules the heart. If at all possible do not allow an operation on the *day* the moon is in a ruling sign of that part of the body on which the operation is to be performed as the results are sometimes not good. It is better if the signs are going away from the affected part than approaching it. Consult the table in Chapter 2 for the body parts ruled by the different signs.

BABIES AND THE SIGNS

To establish the sex of babies divide in half the time between the last day of menstruation to the first day of the next period. If copulation occurs when the moon is in the feminine signs of Pisces, Taurus, Cancer, Virgo, Scorpio, or Capricorn in the first half of the menstrual cycle as noted above, the child is most apt to be female. If copulation occurs when the moon is in the masculine signs of Aquarius, Aries, Gemini, Leo, Libra, or Sagittarius in the last half of the menstrual cycle, except for the last seventy-two hours before menstruation starts again, the child is most likely to be a boy. The seventy-two hours of the last half plus the first half of the new cycle again produces females.

Hazel Berry of Texas says she practically "cut her teeth" on moon signs. Her father farmed by them and her mother always raised her garden by the signs. Hazel believes babies are born "by the moon." For example, if a baby is thought to be due on April 23 and the next change of the moon phase is April 26 then that's when the baby will be born.

Proper weaning is done when the moon is in a zodiac sign that does not rule a vital organ. These signs are Aquarius, Pisces, Sagittarius, and Capricorn. Weaning should not be done when the moon is in any other sign. The last nursing of the child should be done in a fruitful sign.

Chapter 7

FISHING AND HUNTING

The successful country fisherman becomes familiar with the ways of fish. He studies and observes the various habits, traits, and haunts of the types of fish he wants to catch. He becomes an expert on their sense of sight, smell, and hearing. He learns their means of existence, their likes and dislikes, their foods and any other things that will help him to better understand their ways.

The good fisherman must be able to take advantage of their weakness, avoid their keen perception, and outsmart their cunning. Knowing as many things as possible about a certain species of fish helps to locate them. Once located he can then proceed to deceive or tempt them to take his bait.

LAST THINGS FIRST

Instead of waiting until the end of this chapter to give you a summary of country fishing wisdom let's take a look at the most important points right now.

Here are the highlights of how to catch fish, collected from anglers from every part of the country who have spent years studying nature, and fish in particular.

◆ In the summer months the best times to fish are from sunset to one hour after. In the cooler months fishing is best from noon to three in the afternoon. The best day to fish, weatherwise, is a warm, close, cloudy day that follows a bright moonlight night. The most favorable winds are from the south, southwest, and west. East winds are unfavorable.

> "When the wind is in the north
> The skillful fisher goes not forth,
> When the wind is in the south
> It blows the bait in the fishes mouth,
> When the wind is in the east
> 'Tis neither good for man or beast,
> When the wind is in the west
> Then fishing's at its very best."

◆ Use an active lure. With live bait, attach the hook so the bait will have natural movements. With artificial lures, jig or pop the bait and vary the pace of the retrieve.

◆ Present the lure to the water in a manner that will be interesting to the fish both in location and in action. Fish the shady sides of logs and rocks, the down-current sides of boulders and large stumps, and the windless side of ledges and cliffs. Let the bait sink and keep some action going all the time.

◆ Know the fish. Know their patterns of life. What food are they eating right now? When do they feed, and for how long? How do they react when they strike? Polish your techniques to fit the fish.

◆ Fish have a keen sense of sight. Stay out of their range of vision.

◆ Fish have a keen sense of smell. Oil, gasoline, tobacco, onion, and certain other aromas are offensive to fish. Have clean hands, baits, and lures.

◆ Fish have a keen sense of hearing by detecting vibrations. Be as quiet in your movements as possible.

◆ Keep two complete fishing outfits with you at all times. If your line should hang while the fish are biting you can keep catching them without losing any time. Nor will you scare that big one away while trying to release the hung line.

◆ Fish are usually on three levels of most lakes, ponds, and streams. Some are near the surface, some mid-water, and some on the bottom. Work the various levels to find the area of biting fish.

◆ Troll when you can. You can cover large areas to locate fish. You can fish otherwise inaccessible spots. You learn more about the water you are working.

◆ Go with the weather. Sudden barometer changes, fronts, and rising waters often cause fish to start hitting any bait that comes close to them.

- ◆ Position yourself to fish with your back to the wind, and don't allow your shadow to be on the water. In moving water, cast upstream and allow your bait to drift down with the flow.

- ◆ Don't be in a hurry. Give the fish a chance to bite before moving to another spot.

- ◆ Don't quit, keep fishing. Perseverance pays.

FISH FACTS

- ◆ Fish are greedy by nature and will swallow the largest bait they can safely handle. They have a sense as to the size object they can swallow and will go for larger baits up to their maximum swallowing capacity.

- ◆ Fish don't always bite because they are hungry. Sometimes the bait is attractive to them or they bite out of curiosity, greed, or viciousness.

- ◆ Fish need time to turn the bait before they swallow it. Minnows and other bait fish are always swallowed head first.

- ◆ Fish feed on a fairly regular time schedule. If they feed in the early morning they will usually feed again in the late afternoon and then again early the next morning. This will be their regular feeding procedure day after day. Night feeders are equally regular.

- ◆ Brown trout and rainbow trout seem to eat a greater portion of other fish, such as shiners, as they grow larger while smaller trout lean more toward an insect diet.

◆ It is important to know what fish are eating. Often they will feed on only one insect or food for prolonged periods. During these times it is nearly impossible to catch them with any other bait.

◆ Fish have a keen olfactory system. It allows them to have a knowledge of distant things by smell, which is helpful for their feeding and protection.

◆ Fish can taste-test their food before taking it in their mouth by use of sensors on the barbels and fins as well as taste buds in the mouth.

◆ Before and after spawning season fish will eagerly take a variety of baits. Brook trout and many other species will absolutely refuse food during spawning.

◆ Most fish adjust their eyesight to the rhythms of the natural night and day cycle. Any sudden light thrown on them will cause them to leave the area rapidly.

◆ The eyes of fish are placed in such a way that makes it impossible for them to see objects on their level or directly under them. They can, however, see plainly all that is happening above and around them for distances of fifty or more feet.

◆ Shallow water game fish seem to have the best color sense.

◆ Most fish species have a good sense of color perception.

◆ The appearance of a bait seems to be more important than the smell or sound of it.

◆ A very sensitive system of temperature sensation makes it possible for fish to recognize changes of temperature within a fraction of a degree.

◆ A highly developed sense of "touch" helps fish to reject objects that they cannot eat.

◆ The larger the size of a fish the faster it can swim. A general rule is that fish can swim about eight miles per hour for each foot of body length. A fish striking a bait or making any other sudden move can accelerate to about 50 per cent more than its usual cruising speed.

◆ Fish can hear low-frequency sounds from all directions by means of an "ear" inside the head.

FISHING BY THE MOON SIGNS

There seem to be as many theories concerning fishing by the moon signs as there are fishermen. However, from our talks with many anglers we've found most agree to these:

◆ The best signs occur when the moon changes quarters, or when the moon goes into a watery sign (Pisces, Cancer, and Scorpio) or a moist sign (Taurus, Virgo, Libra, and Capricorn). The fish are most active and most likely to bite.

◆ The best period for fishing falls in the period from three days before to three days after a full moon; the day after the full moon is outstanding.

◆ Primo Martinez, a Texas fishing guide for several decades, says "The best time to catch fish is when the moon is directly overhead and the two hours before and two hours after. The next best time is the hour before and the hour after the moon is straight down on the other side of the earth." He says these periods work every time.

◆ The best days of the month, according to information handed down to Louis Viccinelli of Mississippi by old-time fishermen along the Delta, are the two days on either side of the date of the new moon. The first and last quarter phases are also good.

> To fish by the signs always,
> Ya jest can't,
> Ya don't catch no fish
> Where they ain't.

THE WEATHER AND SEASONS

◆ After heavy rains fish often won't bite because plenty of food has washed into the lake.

◆ Fish are hard to catch when fresh snow water is in a stream.

◆ July is generally the worst month for fishing, and June is usually the best fishing month.

◆ Many folks believe that fish possess an instinct which makes it possible for them to feel a coming change in weather. Thomas J. Wheelis, who for many years fished off the rocky coasts of Maine, says, "Three days before dirty weather moves in fish will take the bait almost as soon as it is cast, but on the day of the change of weather they never even come near the lures." He also says that when large fish are swimming near the surface it is a sure sign of coming winds. On the sea he has noted that dolphins and porpoises nearly always announce an approaching storm. They roll, jump, and appear to be "in their happiest hours" just before a great storm. He has also seen whales jump high out of the water in front of wind and storm. Crabs burying themselves deep into the sand is a sure sign of rain and windy weather.

◆ The period immediately following a storm is sometimes the very best of fishing times. The winds stir the water and boil up food from the bottom. This brings in the small fish and behind them come the big fish to get the little ones. Work the shallow waters and be ready for a good catch.

◆ When the air is warm in the spring catfish will swallow almost any bait, alive or dead. On cold days live bait is best. Always allow catfish plenty of time to swallow the hook.

◆ During the summer months black bass go in pairs. If you catch one, try for the mate.

◆ When fishing for black bass it is almost a waste of time to cast on perfectly smooth water.

◆ "Fishing at night is fishing right,
Fishing midday hardly pays,
Dark days are best, they say."

THE LAKE TURNED OVER

When I was just a boy the old-timers would say "the fishing's no good now, the lake just turned over." This seasonal overturn occurs with the coming of spring and with the coming of autumn.

It is interesting to know how this happens. Let's take the fall of the year as an example. Water becomes denser and contracts when it begins to get cool. When the sun drifts toward the south a little each day and the nights show a slight chill in the air, the top layer of water in lakes and ponds begin to cool and become heavy.

The chilled water begins to sink, and the lower layers of warm water start to rise to the top. These layers then become cool and also sink toward the bottom. Thus the water is in a constant state of movement and this churning effect causes the whole body of water to turn completely over. The water becomes muddy and murky as this turning and mixing takes place.

It would make one wonder why the colder water doesn't go straight to the bottom and remain there as a body of cold water. While it is true that as water cools it becomes heavier and denser, this only occurs until it drops to a temperature of 39.2° F. Below 39 degrees, it tends to become lighter in weight.

As it approaches freezing it is so light in weight it starts its journey to the top. In the winter the top water is sometimes frozen into ice and remains in that state until the warmth of spring brings it back to 39 degrees and it again sinks.

LIVE BAIT WISDOM

- ◆ Grub worms are a good general purpose live bait.

- ◆ Small mice make a fine bait for large bass and trout.

- ◆ A live chub or a hellgrammite found under a rock near the river make a good live bass bait.

- ◆ A fine bait in the spring is raw hogs' liver.

◆ Carp like white maggots smeared with honey. Also try stale doughy sweet bread, white potatoes, or a mix of flour, water, and honey rolled into a tight ball. Carp are slow biters so wait until they swim away with the bait before you set the hook.

◆ Bass like live bait such as young carp, small green frogs, and live grasshoppers.

◆ When using frogs for live bait, use small ones and pass the hook through both lips. Keep a bait frog moving by using very small jerks on the line.

◆ When fishing with minnows keep them well under water except in rapid waters when the current will keep the minnow near the surface, which is the right spot for live bait in fast-moving water.

◆ A spoonful of salt or a few drops of iodine in the water bucket will revive sluggish minnows.

◆ An ordinary minnow pail can be aerated to keep minnows alive by using a rubber tube with air bulb attached. Fill the bulb with air and force the air through the water when the minnows appear to get sluggish. This will supply them with the much-needed oxygen to keep them alive for long periods of time.

◆ Bass have a tendency to switch back and forth from insects to fish in their diets but the largest bass will almost exclusively eat fish such as minnows and perch if they are available in quantities to them. Crayfish are a delicacy to bass and if they can be found always give them a try. Don't overlook an eel for bass at night.

◆ Earthworms are one of nature's greatest natural fishing baits. Don't keep them in a tin can, but in an earthen pot (flower pot) or plastic container. Fill it with peat moss or damp green moss, not mud or dirt. Feed them with the white of hard-boiled eggs, a teaspoonful of pure cream, bruised celery, cornmeal, or unmedicated poultry laying mash. They will also eat the powder of finely crushed brick, and although this has no food value a little mixed with their food will give them a healthy red appearance that is attractive to fish. Do not overfeed or overcrowd them.

◆ Use white fat meat shaped like a minnow or frog as a bait for bank fishing.

◆ A fine bait is live maggots taken from fly-blown meat. Some southern fishermen leave fresh meat outdoors for this purpose. Keep the maggots in a small container and feed them cornmeal. Try them on one fishing trip and you'll be convinced.

◆ Keep bait shrimp in wet grass, moss, seaweed, or sawdust.

◆ Check the stomach of fish to know exactly what they are eating at the time you are fishing. They may switch from one form of food to another as it is available, and you can tell by the layers of food in the stomach as to what is in demand. Fish with that bait or something as close to it in size and appearance as possible.

◆ A two-inch strip of brightly colored knitting yarn placed on your hook along with the worm or other live bait sometimes does a good job of attracting fish.

◆ Bring earthworms out of the ground by pouring a mixture of detergent and water over a likely area. Within an hour or so earthworms, garden worms, and nightcrawlers will appear. Any device that will vibrate the ground will also bring them to the surface.

◆ The effectiveness of live bait drops quickly when the bait dies. Place all live baits on your hook with care. Minnows should be hooked through the small part of their body near the tail to miss vital organs. The same is true of worms, hook them as near the tapered end of the tail as possible, or better still, hook them through the tough egg sack band near their head. Hook small frogs through both lips. By following these rules you will have live and active bait much longer.

BAITING HOLES AND ATTRACTING FISH

◆ Fresh meat or cut fish scattered in an area the day before you fish will sometimes bring in the big ones.

◆ A fine fish decoy can be made by placing several big, bright minnows in a clear glass or plastic bottle with a small hole in the top. Suspend the bottle in the water in a likely spot by using a clear monofilament line. The moving, imprisoned minnows will attract fish from a considerable distance.

◆ To attract minnows throw fresh meat scraps and bones in shallow waters and they will hover in the area.

◆ A piece of fresh meat suspended over a fishing hole soon becomes fly blown and drops maggots continually into the water drawing fish.

- A bag of grain or meal, a bale of hay, or a can of dog food with holes punched in the sides makes very good material to bait a fishing hole.

- A drop of anise oil or sweet cicely on your bait can attract fish to it.

- Build a big campfire that reflects upon the water and it will bring fish in at night.

WATER TEMPERATURE

Remember, it always has been and always will be that water temperature is by far the most important single bit of fishing wisdom you need to locate fish. This is a schedule of water temperatures most preferred by various species of fish. Fish will move in and out of these temperature ranges but will spend most of their time in these general zones and 10° on either side of them.

Bass (largemouth)	67–70° F.
Bass (rock)	60–70
Bass (smallmouth)	65–70
Bass (spotted)	73–76
Bass (striped)	55–60
Bass (white)	60–70
Bass (yellow)	64–70
Carp—bottom feeders but prefer	60–75
Catfish—bottom feeders but prefer	62–75
Muskellunge	60–70
Panfish	65–75
Perch (sun and yellow)	60–72
Pickerel	60–65
Pike (northern)	50–70

Salmon (Atlantic)	58–62
Salmon (coho)	52–58
Salmon (landlocked)	43–48
Salmon (Pacific)	52–55
Trout (brook)	55–58
Trout (lake)	45–50
Trout (brown and rainbow)	60–63
Walleye	62–72

Remember, most fish are found in the thermocline temperature area of 60° to 75° F. The 70° to 72° level usually has the heaviest concentrations.

MISCELLANEOUS FISHING SENSE

◆ A good mosquito ointment can be made by mixing ammonia or camphor with tar soap. Crushed pennyroyal weed will also keep these pests away.

◆ When a hook snags your flesh or clothing, push back the upper end and bring the point out the way it went in.

◆ When finned or cut by a fish, clean the wound with clean water and put vinegar on it or put a chew of tobacco on the cut and bind it on for a while.

OTHER WATER CREATURES

◆ Dig clams at the entrance of the wet sign of Libra. Its first week, September 23 to 30, is thought by many moon sign followers to be the best clam digging time. Jewell Honeycutt in Massachusetts watches the weather, the tides, and marks special spots that look good for digging. She then uses this Libra week for harvesting the clams. They are at their best and most plentiful at the time of the full moon.

- When frogging at night use a very bright light, locate the frog, and turn the light into his eyes. He will not jump away and you can pick him up and put him in the bag.

- To catch frogs in the water use a hook and line with a small piece of red rag on the hook. Keep the little frogs for fish bait and fry and eat the frog legs from the big ones.

- Keep frogs in a box with plenty of air holes and some moist moss or grass. Store in a cool place and drench them with water once or twice a day. They will not need food or drink for two or three days.

- Lots of Louisiana folks think the best time to go crabbing is when the moon is full. They use a chicken neck for bait and the crabs bite quickly. The meat will be full and juicy during the full of the moon but at other times the crabs are mostly shell.

HUNTING BY SIGNS AND WEATHER

Libra is the hunter's zodiac sign. Many old-time market hunters, those who would hunt game for sale to others, would only go to the fields and woods when the day sign was in Libra. Rudolph Tierce of Michigan market hunted for over forty years and told me that from records he kept over this long period he could prove that the days the signs were in the loins were the best nine times out of ten.

123

Roy Howell of Florida goes by moon position. He swears that the best hunting occurs when the moon is "the hour on either side of when the moon is overhead, day or night, and when it is calculated to be directly under us on the other side of the earth over China." He thinks this is the time for activity and feeding for most animals if the weather is right.

Ray Humphries of Oklahoma goes by the moon when he hunts deer. He follows the moonlight more than he follows the signs. Ray says that when deer are not disturbed they will feed almost as much in the daytime when the moon is up as they do at night. If the moon shines all night they will feed at night and rest during the day. If the moon is up all day they will feed during those hours and lie quietly at night. During the moon's last quarter, when it has been down and out of sight all day, the deer become very hungry and will range out and feed all night. For still-hunting in the daytime he tries to go when the moon is up or is rising whether it is the morning or afternoon.

Roy Alley of Texas watches the barometer for hunting signs. He says a rising barometer brings game to feeding areas. A falling glass is indicated in the field by upturned tree leaves, showing their light-colored undersides, and often there is possibility of approaching storm. At this time upland birds and most game will desert feeding grounds and go to cover. When the barometer glass begins to fall, Roy turns from deer to ducks. Ducks are most restless at this time and make the best hunting.

Most hunters agree that the wind should be in your face and the sun at your back to have three advantages over the game's wisdom. "They can't smell you, they can't hear as good, and the light favors the hunter instead of the hunted." For the most part, early morning and late evening are considered the best times for all hunting. A good many old and successful hunters still prefer to hunt during the last quarter of the moon, during cold, cloudy weather when the sun is partly hidden.

HUNTING WISDOM

- When the wind is high and the leaves are dry it is a poor time for hunting. Most good hunters agree that a period of steady, light breezes after some rain is the best hunting weather.

- There is a secret to hanging birds and game. Hang birds by the head; hang game by the legs.

- When picking up birds from the water, lift them out by their heads, shake them off and they will be dry. Lifting them by the leg or wing brings water with them and they will be wet and heavy.

- Folks who like to bird hunt, says Milton Beerman of New York, would do well to plant wild rice around ponds and streams in the fall of the year. Ducks and other birds will linger near areas of good feed.

- Soak small game for about twenty-four hours in salt water with a little vinegar added. This both tenderizes the meat and removes the wild taste.

- If it has rained for several days and looks like it will never let up, watch for woodchucks. They follow the sun and will tell you that it will soon clear up enough to bring game out.

- Any animal you hunt is most alert on windy days. Small game burrow up and big game go to heavy ground cover when it is windy. The wise hunter will use wind to his advantage to creep upwind to these hiding places but he must be quiet and remain out of sight as the game will instinctively bed down where they have the best visibility.

Paul Kline of New Jersey has studied ducks and duck hunting for about twenty years. He feels that the best times for shooting are just before daylight and just before dark. Paul would wear a red bandanna handkerchief during duck season, and tie it on a stick and keep himself out of sight while waving it over his head. Ducks have an inquisitive nature and will swim close to investigate unless they are real wild. Paul favors October and November for his duck hunting, on moonlit nights. He works smooth sheltered water when the wind is up and fully believes a good duck hunter should spend more time looking for the favorite feeding and resting spots than in waiting for them to come to you at a blind or to decoys.

Of other birds he says:

- Grouse or partridge hunting is best in the early morning during stormy or cold weather. The best places are around berry bushes or where there is plenty of feed. Learn their roosting places to find them toward night.

- Quail are best found at midday when weather is sunny during October and November. The places are the middles of fields, around brush and stubble, and the edges of woods. A good pointer dog is invaluable.

◆ Woodcock are best hunted in the late evening and at dawn. The best places to hunt are moist lowlands and swamps and the north or wet sides of hills.

◆ Wild geese are very regular in going to and from their feeding grounds. Learn their timetable and get the goose.

TRAPPING

◆ Charlie Frazier of Alaska says that for trapping bear the very best bait he has ever found is fresh fish smeared with honey or burnt honey comb.

◆ Good trappers say that traps should never be handled with bare hands. Cover your hands with rags or use buckskin gloves. Never spit near where traps are set.

◆ One of the best places to place a trap is between two logs with a passageway that animals are apt to pass through.

◆ Drag a piece of fresh raw meat or leave pieces along the ground between your run of traps to lead animals into them.

◆ Never place bait on the trap pan. Always place it above the trap on a stick or hanging from a branch so the animal must step on the trap.

◆ Andy Cefelo of California almost always uses the scent used by many old-time trappers. It is a fish oil scent and he says it works better than any other. He takes trout or fat fish of any kind, cuts them in small pieces and puts them

127

in bottles. Leave these in the hot sun until they become oily and have a putrid smell. Smear this scent on the bait.

◆ Animals are suspicious of a rusty trap. Rustproof them by dipping in a solution of melted beeswax and rosin.

◆ Skunks are the first animals to get prime fur in the late fall and early winter. Water animals are last, bears and badgers have prime fur only in midwinter to early spring.

◆ The best times to trap are the first stormy night of the winter and before any winter storm. The animals are foraging for food and seeking warm holes for dens.

◆ Always sink traps to ground level.

◆ After a catch, leave your trap where it is and reset it. This often pays off again, especially in dens. When sprung traps are found try a new place nearby. If the bait is gone and the trap is unsprung reset it in the same spot, but bait the other side of the trap.

◆ Never dry skins by a fire, as it will spoil them.

◆ I've never tried this one. V. L. Johansen of Utah says old trappers put their hands in skunk holes and pull them out by the tail, hitting them with a club as soon as their head appears. According to the old-timers they will not bite and will not throw their scent at this time.

◆ According to J. E. Westbrook in Colorado, when you find a den or hole that is being used, insert your trap well inside, scent the bait well, and cover with leaves. If left outside near the hole, the animal will be suspicious and not usually take the bait.

Appendix

WEIGHTS AND MEASURES

M ost everything you do in the country has a weight or measure associated with it in one way or another; buying and selling, building, planting and harvesting, even counting out the eggs the old hen lays. For this section we have accumulated weights and measures of every kind and description. This is by no means all the measures that exist, but it's a handy reference as almost all of them have a use at one time or another.

WEIGHTS

In our modern civilization we find many odd weights and measures, some which indicate a notable need for scales or measuring implements. For many of these, rather fantastic origins

129

have been given. We know that Charlemagne found different, arbitrary measures of distance in every country, and struck his huge foot to earth, ordering that its length should be the sole standard for the world. It is said that the English standard, the "grain," was originally derived from the average weight of a grain of barley. The inch was determined from the length of three barley corns, round and dry. The weight of the English penny, by act of Henry III, in 1266, was to be equal to that of thirty-two grains of wheat, taken from the middle of the wheat kernel and well dried. Among the nations of the East, we have the "finger's length," from that of the digit, or second joint of the forefinger, the finger's breadth, the palm, the hand, the span, the cubit or length of the forearm, the stretch of the arms, length of the foot, the step or pace, the stone, pack, etc.

Below we give a table showing some of these measures, now only used for special purposes:

A sack of wool is 22 stone, 14 pounds to the stone, or 308 pounds.

A pack of wool is 17 stone, 2 pounds, or 240 pounds, which is considered a pack load for a horse.

A truss of new hay is 60 pounds; old hay, 50 pounds; straw, 40 pounds.

A load of hay is 36 trusses; a bale of hay is 300 pounds; a bale of cotton, 400 pounds; a sack of Sea Island cotton, 300 pounds.

In England, a firkin of butter is 56 pounds. In the United States, a firkin of butter is 50 pounds. Double firkins, 100 pounds.

> 196 pounds=a barrel of flour.
> 200 pounds=a barrel of beef, pork, or fish.
> 280 pounds=a barrel of salt.

3 pounds=1 stone butcher's meat.

7 pounds=1 clove.

2 cloves =1 stone common articles.

2 stone =1 tod of wool.

6½ tods =1 wey of wool.

2 weys =1 sack of wool.

12 sacks =1 last of wool.

240 pounds=1 pack of wool.

DISTANCE

3 inches	=1 palm.	21.8 inches	=1 Bible cubit.
4 inches	=1 hand.	2½ feet	=1 military pace.
6 inches	=1 span.	3 feet	=1 common pace.
18 inches	=1 cubit.	3.28 feet	=1 meter.

MARINERS' MEASURES

6 feet	=	1 fathom
120 fathoms	=	1 cable length
7½ cable lengths	=	1 mile
5,280 feet	=	1 statute mile
6,076.1 feet	=	1 nautical mile

880 fathoms=1 mile. A ship's cable=a chain 120 fathoms, or 720 feet long.

A hair's breadth=one forty-eighth part of an inch.

A knot, or nautical mile=one-sixtieth of a degree; 3 knots=a marine league; 60 knots, or 69½ statute miles=1 degree.

DRY MEASURE

2 quarts=1 pottle	5 quarters=1 load
2 bushels=1 strike	3 bushels=1 sack
2 strikes=1 coom	36 bushels=1 chaldron
2 cooms=1 quarter	

1 cup	=	½ pint
2 pints	=	1 quart
8 quarts	=	1 peck
4 pecks	=	1 bushel
32 quarts	=	1 bushel

1 barrel (cranberries)=5,826 cubic inches

1 barrel (other fruits, vegetables, and dry produce)=7,056 cubic inches=105 dry quarts

1 bushel=a cube measuring 12.90747 inches on each side.

THE STANDARD BUSHEL

The standard is the Winchester bushel, which contains 2,150.42 cubic inches, or 77.627 pounds avoirdupois of distilled water at its maximum density. Its dimensions are 18½ inches diameter inside, 19½ inches outside, and 8 inches deep.

The heaped bushel requires six inches in the height of the cone above the top of the struck bushel, and contains 2,748 cubic inches in all.

A COMPARATIVE SCALE

Chaldron		Bushels		Pecks		Quarts		Pints
1	=	36	=	144	=	1,152	=	2,304
		1	=	4	=	32	=	64
				1	=	8	=	16
						1	=	2

LIQUID MEASURE

1 teaspoonful	=	$\frac{1}{6}$ ounce (oz.)
1 tablespoonful	=	$\frac{1}{2}$ ounce
16 ounces	=	1 pint (pt.)
2 pints	=	1 quart (qt.)
4 quarts	=	1 gallon (gal.)
31½ gallons	=	1 barrel (br.)
firkin	=	9 gallons
liquid barrel	=	32.5 gallons
hogshead	=	63 gallons
tun	=	252 gallons
1 gallon	=	a cube measuring 6.135792 on each side.

WINE MEASURE

18 United States gallons	=	1 runlet
25 English gallons, or	=	1 tierce
42 United States gallons		
2 tierces	=	1 puncheon
52¼ English gallons	=	1 hogshead
63 United States gallons	=	1 hogshead
2 hogsheads	=	1 pipe
2 pipes	=	1 tun
7½ English gallons	=	1 firkin of beer
4 firkins	=	1 barrel

LIQUID OR WINE MEASURE

16 fluid ounces	=	4 gills
4 gills	=	1 pint
2 pints	=	1 quart
4 quarts	=	1 gallon
31½ gallons	=	1 barrel
2 barrels or		
63 gallons	=	1 hogshead

A COMPARATIVE SCALE

Hogshead		Barrels		Gallons		Quarts		Pints		Gills
1	=	2	=	63	=	252	=	504	=	2016
		1	=	31½	=	126	=	252	=	1008
				1	=	4	=	8	=	32
						1	=	2	=	8
								1	=	4

CAN SIZES

Buffet or picnic	1 cup
No. 1	1¾ cup
No. 1, tall	2 cups
No. 2	2½ cups
No. 2½	3½ cups
No. 3	4 cups
No. 5	7 cups
No. 10	13 cups

SURVEYOR'S LONG MEASURE

7.92 inches=1 link   100 links (66 ft.)=1 chain
25 links=1 rod   80 chains=1 mile
4 rods=1 chain

AREA OR SQUARE MEASURE

144 square inches = 1 square foot
9 square feet = 1 square yard
30¼ square yards = 1 square rod
272½ square feet = 1 square rod
40 square rods = 1 rood, or quarter acre
160 square rods = 1 acre
4 roods = 1 acre
640 acres = 1 square mile or section
43,569 square feet = 1 acre

SURVEYORS' SQUARE MEASURE

625 square links = 1 square rod
16 square rods = 1 square chain
10 square chains = 1 acre
640 acres = 1 square mile
36 square miles
(six miles square) = 1 township

A COMPARATIVE SCALE

Acre		Roods		Rods		Square Yards		Square Feet		Square Inches
1	=	4	=	160	=	4,840	=	43,560	=	6,272,640
		1	=	40	=	1,210	=	10,890	=	1,568,160
				1	=	30¼	=	272½	=	39,204
						1	=	9	=	1,296
								1	=	144

SQUARE FEET AND FEET SQUARE

Never make the mistake of supposing that *square feet* and *feet square* are the same; one foot, yard, rod, or mile, etc., square; or one square foot, yard, rod, mile, etc. are the same, but when beyond the unit measure, the difference increases with the square of the surface, thus:

Fractions of an Acre	Square Feet	Feet Square
$\frac{1}{16}$	2,722½	52½
⅛	5,445	73¾
¼	10,890	104½
½	21,780	147½
1	43,560	208¼
2	87,120	295¼

NOTE: 43,560 square feet=4,840 square yards=1 acre
A square 208.71 feet on all sides=1 acre

HOW TO COMPUTE CAPACITY OF CORN BINS, CRIBS, AND PILED CORN

Husked Ear Corn—The formulas below give answers in bushels of husked ear corn.

Unhusked Ear Corn—Take ⅔ of figure for husked ear corn—unhusked corn varies greatly.

Shelled Corn—Double the number of bushels of husked ear corn.

Corn-cob Mix (Combine run shelled corn and ground cobs)—Figure at approximately same volume as husked ear corn.

137

Square or Rectangular Cribs—Multiply the length by the width by the depth of grain (all in feet). Multiply this sum by 2 and divide by 5. Result is capacity of bushels of husked ear corn at 70 pounds per bushel (15.5 per cent moisture).

Round Cribs—Multiply the diameter by the diameter. Multiply this sum by the depth (all in feet). Multiply the sum by .315 for husked ear corn.

Piled Corn—When heaped in the form of a cone, multiply the diameter by the diameter. Multiply this sum by the depth of the pile at its greatest depth (all in feet). Multiply this sum by .105 for husked ear corn.

CONTENTS OF CRIBS

In the West, and wherever dent corn is raised, three heaping half-bushels are roughly estimated to make a bushel of shelled corn of fifty-six pounds. In reality, sixty-eight pounds of ears of sound dent corn, well dried in the crib, will do so. Four heaping half-bushels of flint corn are allowed for a bushel. One rule for finding the contents is to multiply the length, breadth, and height (in feet) together to obtain cubic feet; multiply this product by four, strike off the right-hand figure, and the result will be nearly the number of shelled bushels.

When the crib is flared both ways, multiply half the sum of the bottom breadths in feet by the perpendicular height in feet, and the same again by the length in feet; multiply the last product by .63 for heaped bushels of ears, and by .42 for the number of bushels in shelled corn. This rule is based on the generally accepted estimate that three heaped half-bushels of ears, or four evenly full, form one bushel of shelled corn.

Length		10	12	14	16	20	24	28	30 ft.
Breadth in feet	3	135	162	189	216	270	324	378	405 bu.
"	4	180	216	252	288	360	432	504	540 bu.
"	5	225	270	315	360	450	510	630	675 bu.
"	6	270	324	378	432	540	648	756	810 bu.
"	7	315	378	441	504	630	756	882	945 bu.
"	8	360	432	504	576	720	864	1008	1080 bu.
"	10	450	540	589	720	900	1080	1260	1350 bu.
"	12	540	648	756	864	1080	1296	1512	1620 bu.

The table above is based on the supposition that the crib is ten feet high, that the breadth is constant, or, if flared, constant half way from the bottom to the top and figuring 3,840 cubic inches of ears to the bushel of shelled corn. Thus a crib 5 feet wide, 10 feet high and 30 feet long will contain 675 bushels of shelled corn.

CONTENTS OF GRANARIES

To find the contents of granaries, multiply length, breadth, and height together to get the cubic feet. Divide this by 56, multiply by 45, and the result will be struck measure. The following table will give the capacities of grain bins, etc. 10 feet high.

139

Width in feet	Bin 6 feet long	Bin 8 feet long	Bin 10 feet long	Bin 12 feet long	Bin 14 feet long	Bin 16 feet long	Bin 20 feet long
	Bu.	Bu.	Bu.	Bu.	Bu.	Bu.	Bu.
3	145	192	241	289	338	386	482
4	193	257	321	386	450	514	643
5	241	321	402	482	563	643	804
6	290	386	482	579	675	771	964
7	338	450	563	675	788	900	1,125
8	386	514	643	771	900	1,029	1,286
9	434	579	723	868	1,013	1,157	1,446
10	482	643	804	964	1,125	1,286	1,607
11	531	707	884	1,061	1,238	1,414	1,768
12	579	771	964	1,157	1,350	1,542	1,920

CONTENTS OF CISTERNS

Thirty-six inches of rain per year will yield 72 barrels of water for each 10 foot square (100 square feet) of roof. Thus a 30′ by 40′ barn may supply 2 barrels per day throughout the year. In dry areas that is, areas where heavy rains are succeeded by long dry spells the cisterns must be larger than where rains are more constant. When the water is to be used daily a 30′ by 40′ barn should have a cistern 10 feet in diameter and 9 feet deep; this will hold 168 barrels. But if the water is to be drawn from only in time of drouth, it should be three times this capacity.

To determine the contents of a circular cistern of equal size at top and bottom, find the depth and diameter in inches; square the diameter and multiply the square by the decimal .0034, which will find the quantity of gallons for 1 inch in depth. Multiply this by the depth in inches, divide by 31½, and the result will be the number of barrels the cistern will hold. The following table shows the number of barrels of liquid the following diameters will hold, for each 12 inches in depth:

5 feet	diameter,	capacity	per	foot,	in depth,	=	4.66	barrels.
6 "	"	"	"	"	"		6.71	"
7 "	"	"	"	"	"		9.13	"
8 "	"	"	"	"	"		11.93	"
9 "	"	"	"	"	"		15.10	"
10 "	"	"	"	"	"		18.65	"

To find the contents of a square cistern, multiply the length by the breadth, multiply this result by 1,728 and divide the total by 231. The result will be the number of gallons for each foot in depth. The following table shows the barrels for the sizes named for square cisterns:

5 feet by	5 feet	has capacity	per foot	in depth of		5.92	barrels.
6 "	6 "	"	"	"		8.54	"
7 "	7 "	"	"	"		11.63	"
8 "	8 "	"	"	"		15.19	"
9 "	9 "	"	"	"		19.39	"
10 "	10 "	"	"	"		23.74	"

LAND MEASURE

Farmers often wish to know the contents of a field. To find the number of acres in any square or rectangular field, multiply the length in rods and breadth in rods together, and divide by

160; or, multiply the length in feet by breadth in feet and divide by 43,560, the number of square feet in an acre. Thus:

10 rods by 16 rods=	1 acre
8 rods by 20 rods=	1 acre
5 rods by 32 rods=	1 acre
4 rods by 40 rods=	1 acre
5 yards by 968 rods=	1 acre
10 yards by 484 yards=	1 acre
20 yards by 242 yards=	1 acre
40 yards by 121 yards=	1 acre
80 yards by 60½ yards=	1 acre
70 yards by 69½ yards=	1 acre
220 feet by 198 feet=	1 acre
440 feet by 99 feet=	1 acre
110 feet by 369 feet=	1 acre
60 feet by 726 feet=	1 acre
120 feet by 363 feet=	1 acre
240 feet by 181½ feet=	1 acre
200 feet by 108.9 feet=	½ acre
100 feet by 145.2 feet=	⅓ acre
100 feet by 108.9 feet=	¼ acre
43,560 square feet=	1 acre
4,840 square yards=	1 acre

USEFUL RULES

To find the number of gallons in a cylindrical tank—Multiply the square of the diameter in inches by .7854, and multiply this product by the height, in inches, then divide the result by 231.

To find the number of tons of hay in long square stacks—

Multiply the length in yards by the width in yards, and that by half the altitude in yards, and divide the product by 15.

To find the contents of boards, in square feet—Multiply the length (in feet), by the width (in inches), and divide the product by 12.

Find contents of a 16-foot board, 9 inches wide—9 by 16= 144÷12=12 square feet.

Of an 18-foot board, 13 inches wide—13 by 18=234÷12= 19½ square feet.

To find the contents of scantlings, joists, sills, etc. in square feet—Multiply the length, width, and thickness together, and divide product by 12.

To find the contents of granaries, wagon beds in bushels— Multiply the number of cubic feet by .8 (for greater accuracy by .8036). A wagon bed 3 feet wide and 10 feet long will hold 2 bushels for every inch in depth.

Corn Cribs—Good quality ear corn, measured when settled, will hold out at 2¼ cubic feet per bushel. Inferior quality, 2⅜ to 2½ cubic feet per bushel.

Hay—The quantity of hay in a mow or stack can only be ap- proximately ascertained by measurement. It takes about 350 cubic feet of well-settled timothy hay to make a ton; from 400 to 450 cubic feet of partly settled hay.

Haystacks—To find contents of a round stack in cubic feet, multiply the square of the average circumference by the average height, and this product by .08; then divide by 350 if the hay is well settled, by 400 or 450 otherwise.

For an oblong-shaped stack, multiply the average length, width and height together, and divide by the same figures.

Coal—Hard coal in the solid state averages about 80 pounds per cubic foot, or 25 cubic feet to a ton. Chestnut-size lumps average about 56 pounds per cubic foot.

Cord Wood—A cord of wood is a pile 4 feet wide, 4 feet high and 8 feet long, and contains 128 cubic feet. Hence, to find the contents of a pile of wood, in cubic feet and cords, multiply length, width, and thickness together, and divide by 128.

Stone—A perch of stone masonry is 16½ feet long, 1½ feet high and 1 foot thick, and contains 24¾ cubic feet.

To find the contents of a wall, in perches, find the number of cubic feet, then divide by 24¾ (or multiply by .0404).

INDEX